ADMINISTRATIVE REFORMS in BANGLADESH

SAP Library on South Asia

Bhutan: The Political Economy of Development
Gautam Kumar Basu, 184 pp., 1995, cloth
Religion, Politics and Communalism:The South Asian Experience
Rakhahari Chatterji, 184 pp., 1994, cloth
Framing South Asian Transformation
An Examination of Regional Views on South Asian Cooperation
Naren Chitty, 184 pp., 1994, cloth
Why Alliances Endure: The United States-Pakistan Alliance
Rekha Datta, 228 pp., 1994, cloth
Security Dilemma of a Small State
Part I Sri Lanka in South Asian Context
P.V.J. Jayasekera, 536 pp., 1992, cloth
Part II Internal Crisis and External Intervention in Sri Lanka
P.V.J. Jayasekera and M. Werake, 424 pp., 1995, cloth
Changing Face of Nationalism: The Case of Bangladesh
Muhammad Ghulam Kabir, 249 pp., 1994, cloth
New Dimensions of Government and Policts in Nepal
P.D. Kaushik, 276 pp., 1996, cloth
Ahmadiya Community in Pakistan
Surendra Nath Kaushik, 164 pp., 1996, cloth
Clinton Administration and South Asia
V.K. Malhotra, 186 pp., 1997, cloth
Conduct of India's Foreign Policy
K.D. Mathur and P.M. Kamath, 183 pp., 1996, cloth
National Interest and Foreign Policy
Golam Mostafa, 248 pp., 1995, cloth
Understanding South Asia
S.D. Muni, 238 pp., 1994, cloth
Socio-Economic Profile of SAARC Countries
T. Nirmala Devi, 168 pp., 1994, cloth
Population and Development in SAARC
T. Nirmala Devi, 140 pp., 1996, cloth
Islam in South Asia: A Regional Perspective
Asim Roy, 223 pp., 1996, cloth
Politics of Tamil Nationalism in Sri Lanka
Ambalavanar Sivarajah, 248 pp., 1996, cloth
The Zia Episode in Bangladesh Politics
Habib Zafarullah, 216 pp., 1996, cloth

ADMINISTRATIVE REFORMS IN BANGLADESH

Mohammad Mohabbat Khan
Department of Public Administration
University of Dhaka, Dhaka 1000, Bangladesh

South Asian Publishers ♦ New Delhi

SOUTH ASIAN PUBLISHERS PVT. LTD.
50 Sidharth Enclave, P.O. Jangpura, New Delhi 110014

ISBN 81-7003-214-8

Typeset at Anjali Computer Typesetting
50 Sidharth Enclave, PO. Jangpura, New Delhi 110014
[Phones: 6925315; 6835713]

Published by South Asian Publishers Pvt. Ltd.
50 Sidharth Enclave, P.O. Jangpura, New Delhi 110014
and printed at
Mehra Offset Press, Chandni Mahal, Daryaganj
New Delhi 110002.
Printed in India.

DEDICATION

This book is dedicated to all my students at the Universities of Chittagong, Dhaka, Southern California, Benin and Yarmouk in Bangladesh, USA, Nigeria and Jordan. I have learned a lot from my students during my twenty-seven years of university teaching in a number of countries and this dedication is an acknowledgment and a humble effort to repay that debt.

Contents

Preface

The dominant role of bureaucracy in governance in Bangladesh is recognized readily by politicians, academics and citizens at large. Bangladesh has been and continues to be an administrative state where civil servants have played a critical role both in policy making and policy implementation. Public pronouncements notwithstanding, politicians in power have had to depend heavily on the expertise of the civil servants. Weak political institutions, controversy over the form and working of governments, lust for power and leadership have all contributed to bureaucratic dominance over state affairs. Accountability mechanisms of civil servants have failed. Transparency in public decision making at all levels is conspicuous by its absence. Public service as a whole is vitiated by inter-cadre rivalries, groupism and unionism. All these symptoms of deep-rooted malices are evident to anyone who observes functioning of public servants. This is far from a desirable state of affairs.

The need for reforming the bureaucracy was recognized a long time ago even before the birth of Bangladesh as an independent country. From the very beginning in united Pakistan committees and commissions were appointed to discern the ills afflicting the public service. Those reform bodies came up with sound and well-reasoned measures to decisively change the nature and structure of public service system and ethos of public servants. In independent Bangladesh the same trend of appointing committees and commissions with distinguished individuals to study the public service is noticeable. But the major recommendations of such bodies were either not at all implemented or implemented in such a manner so that the intended outcome failed to materialize.

The present book is an attempt to understand, describe and analyse why major administrative reforms failed in Bangladesh; what lessons can be learned from such failure; and how major reforms can be effectuated within the civil service system of this country. To succeed in such an ambitious task is difficult indeed. That is why an endeavour is made here to look at administrative reform from a global perspective focusing both on theoretical as well as recent practical developments in the area. Also bureaucratic culture has been discussed both conceptually as well as its manifestation in Bangladesh context. Selected dimensions of civil service which have relevance to reform have also been analysed. Major administrative reform efforts of five effective rulers of Bangladesh have been critically evaluated. Role of four international donors in the area of public service reform has also been analysed. Lastly, lessons from Bangladesh's experience with major administrative reforms have been examined with reference to other commonwealth countries and specific measures have been recommended to bring about major administrative reforms in the public service system of Bangladesh.

The book draws on my earlier work *Politics of Administrative Reform: The Case of Bangladesh* (New Delhi: Ashish, 1991). But excepting chapter two all other chapters in the book are new and written specifically for the present volume keeping in mind new developments in the areas of bureaucracy and major administrative reforms in Bangladesh and elsewhere.

November 1997 Mohammad Mohabbat Khan
Dhaka 1000

Acknowledgement

The author is grateful to scholars and practitioners in the area of administrative reform whose ideas and knowledge he has used in writing this book. They are too numerous to be mentioned here by names. Professor Gerald E. Caiden remains the single source of inspiration for the author. My former students Professor Habib M. Zafarullah of the University of New England, Professor Nizamuddin Ahmed of the University of Chittagong and Dr. Mohammad Habibbur Rahman of the University of Dhaka inspired me to complete this book. Dr. A. T. M. Obaidullah of Rajshahi University also encouraged me to write this book. Professor M. Anisuzzaman formerly of the University of Chittagong and Professor Emajuddin Ahamed of the University of Dhaka made several useful suggestions and comments on my earlier book *Politics of Administrative Reform: The Case of Bangladesh* which helped me to write this new book.

I am grateful to my wife Rokeya Khan for providing me with both emotional and other support during writing of this book. My two sons Asheq Khan and Imran Khan allowed me the time to concentrate on the work of this book by sacrificing their demand on my time.

Mohammad Somiruddin Mollah typed the entre manuscript on the computer and Ahmed Sarwerruddawla supervised typing of the manuscript. I appreciate the efforts of both of them in completing the work.

CHAPTER 1

Globalization of Administrative Reform

INTRODUCTION

Administrative reform (AR) is a widely used concept. Still disagreement persists among scholars and practitioners as to the meaning, nature, strategies and outcome of AR. In spite of such disagreements governments in all developing regions have long realized that effective public administration systems are essential to the achievement of national development objectives (UN, 1983:1). There is a sustained consciousness among these countries of the continuing urgency of major administrative reforms (UN, 1982: 13). It has also become imperative to differentiate between major administrative reforms and minor improvements in public administration system in a particular country. Major administrative reforms are undertaken usually in response to significant social, political or functional changes while the latter emerge as a continuing process of evolution in response to changing requirements (UN, 1981:15). Increasingly, open recognition is being given to the fact that structural and process reforms are less demanding than normative and attitudinal factors in making public services more effective as agents of change (UN, 1982:13). This chapter (a) presents some definitions of AR and analyses the representative definitions from among them; (b) discusses the continuing importance of AR in the present context of developing countries; (c) probes into the constraints to AR; (d) delineates some of the key strategies for facilitating AR; and (e) focuses on some of the major recent trends and developments pertaining to AR in the 1990s and beyond.

DEFINING ADMINISTRATIVE REFORM

The wide divergence that exists among scholars regarding the meaning of administrative reform and its consequences was pointed out in late '60s by the foremost theoretician of administrative reform this way:

> The study of administrative reform is handicapped by the absence of a universally accepted definition. The indiscriminate use of the term has led to confusion and to difficulties in setting parameters for research and theorizing . . . The term has been applied, for instance, to all improvements in administration . . . to general administrative overhauls in difficult circumstances . . . to specific remedies for maladministration . . . to any suggestion for better government (Caiden, 1969:4).

Caiden's observations made almost thirty years ago remains valid even today. One of the first scholars who attempted to understand and define the concept of AR was Caiden. For him it means 'the artificial inducement of administrative transformation against resistance' (Caiden, 1969:65). Administrative Reform, according to Caiden, contains three interrelated properties: moral purpose (which points to the need for improving the status quo), artificial transformation (which leads to a considerable departure from existing arrangements), and administrative resistance (when opposition is assumed) (Caiden, 1969:65). This definition has been interpreted by Anisuzzaman and Khan this way: (1) that AR is subject to human design (artificial) and it involves persuasion, argument and advocacy as opposed to force (inducement), (2) that it leads to or is part of a change (transformation); and which (3) generates some opposition to the change proposed (resistance) (Anisuzzaman and Khan, 1980:29). A practitioner interprets Caiden's definition of AR more or less in similar vein as Anisuzzaman and Khan do. For him the definition implies that (1) administrative reform is artificially stimulated by man and is not accidental, automatic or natural; (2) administrative reform is a transformatory process; and (3) resistance is a concomitant of the process of administrative reform (Dey, 1971:560). Quah questions the definition of Caiden on three grounds: (1) it does not indicate the goals of administrative reform; (2) it does not provide an adequate description of the content of administrative reform; and (3) the element of resistance is not a distinguishing feature of administrative reform (Quah, 1981:39).

Lee views administrative reform as a complex process in which many factors interact and affect one another and whose results can be found over a considerable period of time (Lee, 1970). He states that AR 'is an effort to apply new ideas and combination of ideas to administrative system with a conscious view to improving the system for positive goals of development' (Lee, 1970:7). He contributes two concepts, i.e. (a) new ideas are necessary and related to improving the system; and (b) whose application is related to the positive goals of national development (Lee, 1976). Lee's definition of AR does two things : (a) it gives AR a national dimension as distinguished from purely organizational or intrabureaucratic concerns for change; and (2) usefulness of innovation in AR is assumed to be related to the improvement of the administrative system (Anisuzzaman and Khan, 1980:33).

Dror defines AR as 'directed change of the main features of an administrative reform, a case of directed administrative system, change must either (a) be at least of medium comprehensiveness plus high innovativeness; or (b) be of high comprehensiveness plus at least medium innovativeness (Dror, 1976). But his definition suffers from a vagueness arising out of his inability or unwillingness to delineate the main features of an administrative system as well as what constitutes an AR (Anisuzzaman and Khan, 1980:35).

Definitions of AR provided by Caiden, Lee and Dror are useful but limitations of their efforts are now widely recognized. Below some definitions of AR are presented which will enable one to better understand and operationalize the concept.

Reform is generally identified with 'improvement' or the creation of good administration (Saxena, 1980:18). To Leemans it (reform) has consequently acquired normative taint (Leemans, 1976:13). Thus AR refers to 'changes of broad scope and high intensity in the governmental organization' (Leemans, 1976). It has been argued that AR will include the reorganization of the machinery of government as a sub-system of the larger system containing political and bureaucratic elements (Leemans, 1976). He adds that 'success or failure of reform again depends largely on the influence and power structure in the organization and on the influence and power of persons and groups who support or oppose the reorganization. It is unlikely that reform action will affect the reorganization process unless it has the support of people or groups who can exercise a good deal of influence' (Leemans, 1976). Mukarjee agrees that 'the opportunities of change and its dimensions could conceivably be stretched by winning supporters in centres of influence, both political and administrative' (Mukarjee, 1971). It needs to be pointed out here that it is not accurate to use reform and reorganization as interchangeable words as Leemans has done. It is probably more accurate to say that administrative reorganization constitutes one important procedure for implementing administrative reforms (Quah, 1981:31). More pertinently, administrative reform can be differentiated from reorganization this way. The broader term 'administrative reform' usually implies a crusading intent; it has a definite moralistic tone. In content, it may actually involve 'reorganization' and 'innovation' (Abueva, 1970:21).

The discussion above sets the tone for analyzing below those definitions of AR that are more appropriate for the purpose of this book.

Administrative reform can be defined as the 'deliberate use of authority and influence to apply new measures to an administrative system so as to change its goals, structures and procedures with a view to improving it for developmental purposes' (UN,

1983:1). This definition to a large extent portrays the dynamics of AR. But its lack of emphasis on attitudinal aspects of civil servants considerably weakens its appeal.

Quah defines AR as 'a deliberate attempt to change both (a) the structure and procedure of public bureaucracy (i.e., reorganization or the institutional aspect) and (b) the attitudes and behaviour of the public bureaucrats involved (i.e., the attitudinal aspect), in order to promote organizational effectiveness and attain national development goals' (Quah, 1981:44). Though this definition quite appropriately includes structures and procedures of public organizations along with attitudes and behaviours of public officials as targets of conscious change, but it also links at the sametime such change with commitment for national development. This linking of national development with AR and inclusion of reorganization within AR makes Quah's definition too broad and cumbersome and difficult to accept in totality.

Abueva offers a definition of AR that is useful for our purpose here. He views AR 'essentially as a deliberate attempt to use power, authority and influence to change the goals, structure or procedures of the bureaucracy, and therefore to alter the behaviour of its personnel' (Abueva, 1970:22). He further amplifies the definition by adding that AR 'aims to change or redirect the characteristic or conventional ways by which people in the government think and act vis-a-vis each other, towards the organizations they may be representing and in relation to individual citizens as well as to various segments of the public' (Abueva, 1970). Abueva's definition is both comprehensive as well as specific.

Khan's definition of AR is very similar to that of Abueva. He defines AR as 'those efforts which call for or lead to major changes in the bureaucratic system of a country intended to transform the existing and established practice, behaviours and structures within it' (Khan, 1980:57). Khan's definition along with those of Abueva, UN and partially Quah's will be utilized to understand, interpret and evaluate major administrative reform initiatives in Bangladesh.

IMPORTANCE OF ADMINISTRATIVE REFORM

Redesigning and overhauling the structure and organization of governmental apparatuses as well as modifying and changing the behavioural patterns of public servants have been, in most cases, the continuing concerns of administrative reformers all over the world. These concerns are premised on three fundamental beliefs about limitations of public organizations. These are: the imperfectability of human institutions, the conservative nature of large public organizations, and the slowness of innovations to permeate public organizations (Caiden, 1985:459). These premises on the one hand point to the crucial and omnipresent role of administrative reform in the field of public administration as well as underscore the importance of appropriate and timely implementation of major administrative reform measures to improve delivery of public services, to enforce greater accountability of public servants to political leaders in power and to increase the accessibility of citizens to public offices. The persistent concern with administrative reforms in general and major administrative reforms in particular in developing countries can be attributed to: discontinuities between a colonial administrative system and the needs and demands of sovereign governments, another to the need for an administrative apparatus adequate for performing the expanding role of governments in managing the economy, and the third to the desire to change the orientation and attitudes of civil servants and to introduce modern management techniques or processes in order to make the administration more efficient and effective in the delivery of services to the public (UN, 1983:3).

CONSTRAINTS TO MAJOR ADMINISTRATIVE REFORMS

Still many constraints have made initiation and more so implementation of major administrative reforms difficult in the countries of Africa, Asia and the Middle East. These constraints can be summarized as follows:

> (a) reform measures have been ill-conceived and are unclear about their objectives; (b) administrative reforms efforts have not been integrated with socio-economic developments; (c) administrative reform efforts have been politically motivated and often geared to partisan or individual rather than overall national interests; (d) resistance towards reforms is generated and sustained by civil servants who perceive their interest to be adversely affected as a result of implementation of proposed reforms; (e) lack of professionalism among civil servants, who handle administrative reform, denied it (administrative reform) the necessary disciplined and systematic approach; (f) lack of adequate and sustained institutional support for administrative reform; (g) persistence phenomenon of administrative dependence, i.e. on colonial administrative system which is not in tune and sometimes in conflict with indigenous institutions, social customs and values; (h) prevalence of excessive formalism resulting in overconcentration and evaluating formal organizational structures, designing new ones and institutionalizing the legal basis for their implementation, and (i) insufficient public support for reform (UN, 1982:14; UN, 1979: 29-30)

But major limitations of administrative reforms have usually surfaced during the implementation stage. Caiden has catalogued a long list of practical problems which resulted in the failure of major administrative reform proposals and measures. These include:

> (a) a bad beginning, where the reformers did not have sufficient grasp of the situation to realize that they were unacceptable or their reforms were unworkable or they merely reinforced existing deficiencies by advocating more of the same; their reforms were stillborn; (b) imitation not innovation, where reforms were exact copies of what had succeeded elsewhere but would fail in this particular situation or would remain unimplemented as ritual affirmation of administrative ethics because people already knew what to do but they did not know how to do it; (c) incorrect diagnosis, where reformers misinterpreted the facts or got sidetracked into inconsequential or they accepted too much without question; (d) hidden intentions, where the reformers had or were suspected of having hidden agendas of their own and no one would cooperate with them as a result; (e) indecisive approach, where the reformers could not agree even among themselves as to the scope, magnitude of change, rate of

change and comprehensiveness of their proposals, and failed to convince people that they were serious; (f) faulty planning, where the reformers could not operationalize, where the reformers were overly conservative in their choice of strategies, switched from macro-reforms to technical trivia, and failed to attract creative talent and transform it into a critical mass of congenial reform advocates; (h) inability to command resources; (i) no monitoring, which meant that the reformers did not know to what extent their reforms were being modified or altered; (j) absence of feedback, which meant that the reformers had no idea what was really happening at all; (k) evaluation ignored, which meant that the reformers did not know whether their reforms were actually working or doing the things they were supposed to do; and (l) goal displacement, where the intention of the reformers were subordinated to other objectives, and administrative reform was only a pretext for political, social, cultural and economic change (Caiden, 1976:145-165 quoted inBjur and Caiden, 1981:114-115).

STRATEGIES FOR FACILITATING MAJOR ADMINISTRATIVE REFORMS

Devising strategies for facilitating implementation of major administrative reforms is not an easy task given the complex and difficult job of bringing about wide-ranging changes in well-entrenched and tradition-bound civil services in developing countries.

The studies commissioned as well as undertaken by the United Nations have put forward a number of strategies to overcome the myriad of problems which characterize the reform process. These strategies are:

(a) fostering an environment favourable to reform, facilitated by the right political, social and administrative climate, derived from an awareness of the urgency for administrative reform; (b) appointing a high-level commission with representation of all interests from time to time to undertake a comprehensive review of the public services, to identify the major administrative deficiencies and to advice on the appropriate reform measures to be undertaken; (c) devising of comprehensive plans and programmes, flexible and easy to implement, for administrative reform on the advice of the commission proposed above and its acceptance or modifications by the government; (d) integration of all administrative reform measures with national socio-economic plans and making the former consistent with overall development objective; (e) creation of a permanent machinery comprising of a network of implementing organs in the different sectors, departments and levels of government to ensure proper implementation of administrative reform measures; and (f) redirecting personal attitudes, motivations and professional values of the civil servants to make them more change-oriented (UN, 1982: 14-15; UN, 1979: 30 - 31).

Wilenski highlights some very important basic rules to facilitate implementation of administrative reforms. These rules combine in them elements of both reform objectives and a reform strategy. They are:

identify and publicize the failure of public bureaucracies so as to reinforce existing dissatisfaction;
recognize that there will be resistance to reform so that strategy must build alliance with key individuals or groups and if possible pit one part of the bureaucracy against another;
devote greater attention to implementation and place lesser emphasis on formulating a policy reform, ideally the two processes should be integrated;
identify or choose effective levels of change like enactment of new legislation, creating a new institution that will bring about change in administrative behaviour;
other levers of change could include bringing in new people, changing formal processes and formal organization structures (Wilenski, 1986: 257-276).

Caiden, after analyzing the existing literature and experiences of many countries specially those in the developing areas, presents a number of variables and conditions which paved the way for successful implementation of major administrative reforms.

First, reforms were political in character and intended to strengthen direct governmental control over public service by changing the power and influence of the latter. Second, the government was deter-

> mined to impose radical reform measures in the face of resistance by civil servants provided by such measures had the support of the technical experts and people-at-large. Third, civil servants were involved at every stage of the reform cycle, i.e., from planning to implementation, to ensure their support in the reform exercise. Fourth, reform goals were set in such a manner so that these could be achievable as well as measurable with the intention of learning quickly of the outcome and adopting necessary corrective measures. Fifth, reform concentrated on utilizing existing arrangements and selected instruments to show confidence in civil servants. Sixth, reform leaders had a deep personal interest in the fate of the reforms. Seventh, the reformers were always aware of the inherent limitations of their efforts (Caiden, 1988:353).

MAJOR TRENDS IN ADMINISTRATIVE REFORM IN THE 1990s AND BEYOND

Civil services in many developing countries are even today too large, too expensive and insufficiently productive; and civil servants, especially those in the managerial positions are poorly motivated (Nunberg and Nellis, 1990:2). This is a sad commentary on the state of administrative reform after four decades of continuous experimentation with new ideas, quick-fix methods and fail-proof strategies. Several international donors/bodies like the World Bank and the International Monetary Fund, the United Nations and the Commonwealth Secretariat have spent lot of resources on experts to come up with solutions of multifarious ills afflicting the civil service systems all over the world.

> Their agendas include liberalization, deregulation, downsizing the public sector, shrinking bloated public organizations, privatization, debureaucratization, civil service reform, budget reform, performance measures, businesslike management, long-term transparency, efficiency and accountability (Caiden, 1991).

The above-mentioned agendas had striking similarities with the important approaches tried out in Anglo-American democracies in the 1980s to reform the civil service.

> . . . the assumption of public sector inefficiency, the recourse to private sector expertise, the stubborn belief in the usefulness of merit pay and the tremendous emphasis on new accounting procedures (Pollitt, 1985:45).

The decade of the '90s has already seen emergence of a number of approaches that attempt to bring about improvements in the efficiency, effectiveness and performance in the public sector. These approaches have been hailed by many as provider of appropriate remedies to a discredited public sector. At the sametime, some have questioned the validity of these approaches in the context of public sector which, according to them, is significantly different from the private sector. The discussion below attempts to describe the major tenets of three new approaches: citizen's charter, re-engineering and reinventing government. It needs to be stated that there are some important differences among three approaches in terms of emphasis on principles and ideas.

CITIZEN'S CHARTER

As of now the significant developments have taken place in the British civil service with the launching of the Citizen's Charter in July 1991. The Charter aimed at 'raising the standard of public services by making them more responsive to the wishes and needs of the users' (The Citizens's Charter, 1991:5). The end-product expected to include high quality services provided efficiently and at a reasonable cost. The Citizens' outlines six important principles which are designed to emphasize the idea of citizen as a customer of public services and transform it (the idea) into a reality in every day management and operation of those services.

First, explicit and measurable standards for civil service be established and monitored. These standards must be known to the citizens so that they know what services are expected and as to whether standards have been met or not while providing stipulated services. So publication of actual performance against set standards is also required.

Second, it is crucial that complete and accurate information, is readily available and easily accessible about how civil service is run, what it costs, how well it performs and who is in-charge and at what point. Information and openness are needed, among other things, to build rapport and trust between civil servants and members of the public.

Third, within the broad ambit of the public sector citizens should be provided with maximum opportunity to choose, among competing services. It is widely believed that choice, is possibly the best stimulant to improve quality. Regular and systematic consultation must take place between civil servants and users of services. This is because users views about services and their suggestions for improving them are critically important for taking final decisions on standards.

Fourth, the basic premise behind courtesy and helpfulness is that public services should be provided equally and without discrimination or bias to all who are entitled and run it in the manner to suit their convenience.

Fifth, civil servants must always be aware as what to do when things go wrong. The actions to be taken in such situations include offering an unconditional and public apology, a full explanation as to where and how things went out of track and initiating swift and effective measures to remedy the mistakes committed. But things cannot be put right unless compliant procedures are well publicized, in place and easy to deal with. Independent reviews of procedures should be undertaken from time to time to bring them in tune with needs of the users.

Sixth, tax payer is the king is the philosophy behind the value for money (VFM) principle. He should be ensured efficient and economical delivery of services within the resource constraint of the state. One of the prerequisites of VFM is that an independent validation of performance against standards must be undertaken on a continuous basis.

It is imperative from the above discussion that all the principles are interrelated. Standards of performance is critical for choice and consultation, putting things right and value for money. But running through all these principles are the themes of accountability, efficiency, effectiveness, productivity and transparency. In essence, the charter is an agenda about:

> outcomes and outputs, rather than inputs, and the needs of users and not the interests of producers;
> government sticking to essentials and doing those well;
> using markets wherever possible to improve choice and, through the spur of competition, to achieve better value for money;
> addressing the particular task, designing the shape of the organization which best meets it, and delegating responsibility for delivery to that organization;
> raising the performance of individual public servants through effective recruitment, training, appraisal and incentives (Mottram, 1994:3).

Many developing countries reform efforts also indicate a clear shift away from traditional concerns mostly with rules and regulations to increasing emphasis on quality culture, performance targets, contracting out of services, customer orientation, accountability and transparency.

RE-ENGINEERING

Re-engineering as a term was coined by Hammer in 1990 (Hammer, 1990). Re-engineering having its origins in big business in USA is considered to be equally applicable to public organizations.

'Re-engineering is the fundamental rethinking and radical redesign of business processes to achieve dramatic improvements in critical contemporary measures of performance, such as cost, quality, service, and speed' (Hammer and Champy, 1993:32). Re-engineering, according to Kruger (1993:31) as quoted in Halachmi (1995:329-330), is considered a comprehensive and effective way for organizations to reduce cycle times, surpass customer expectations, enhance productivity, increase sales and reap higher profits.

But re-engineering as a concept is yet to be defined precisely to the satisfaction of all. The attempt is on to define and redefine the concept on the basis of results obtained from its applications in various kinds of organizations in different settings. Halachmi (1995:331) has found it more worthwhile to discern the salient attributes of the concept rather than attempt to define it in precise detail. According to him such attributes can be found in the writing of some prominent authors in the area of re-engineering (Hammer and Champy, 1993; Davenport, 1993; Davenport and Short, 1990).

The main attributes of re-engineering are the following (Halachmi, 1995:331). First, the concentration is on developing around processes and outcomes. The preference is to see an individual perform all tasks in the process whenever feasible. Second, the central focus is on the customer or client within a results-oriented and team-based approach. This requires rigorous measurement of performance and close analysis of change and the rate of change for assessing performance. But that is possible with total commitment of all employees and a substantive involvement of top management at all times. Third, systematic searches be undertaken to bring about radical changes for the purpose of improvements and breakthroughs when an incremental approach will not succeed.

REINVENTING GOVERNMENT

Reinventing government has become a very powerful and catchy phrase during last three years. The term was popularized by the publication of an influential book by Osborne and Gaebler titled *Reinventing Government* (1992). The book contains a number of rationales for the reinvention movement. These are: to empower citizens, to promote mission-driven entrepreneurial leadership in order to 'steer rather than row', to enhance competition and deregulate government by cutting red tape, to foster 'total quality management', to decentralize government, and argument for performance budgeting, support for civil service reform and advocacy for privatization (Nathan, 1995:213).

The reinventing government idea has been accepted with great enthusiasm by Clinton Administration in USA President Clinton formed a National Performance Review (NPR) team under the leadership of Vice President Al Gore. The government report titled 'From Red Tape to Results: Creating a Government that Works Better Costs Less' published in 1994 contained 384 specific recommendations and predicted a saving of $ 108 billion for US government over five years if these recommendations were implemented. Gore's exercise sometimes dubbed as 'reinventing the federal government' intended to invent a government that puts people first by (a) serving its customers, (b) empowering its employees, and (c) fostering excellence (Moe, 1994:111). All these would be done by (a) creating a clear sense of mission, (b) delegating authority and responsibility, (c) replacing regulations with incentives, (d) developing budget-based outcomes, and (e) measuring success by customer satisfaction (Moe, 1994:111).

The Gore report is based on what it termed as four bedrock principles of executive branch entrepreneurial management (Moe, 1994: 113). First, effective entrepreneurial governments cast aside red tape, shifting from systems in which people are accountable for following rules to systems in which they are accountable for achieving results. Second, effective entrepreneurial governments insist on customer satisfaction. Third, effective entrepreneurial governments transform their cultures by decentralizing authority. Fourth, effective entrepreneurial governments constantly find way to make governments work better and cost less.

Whatever support the reinventing government idea has generated specially among politicians in USA it has also received its share of criticisms from academics. The criticisms are both practical as well as ideological. It has been pointed out that 'government has never established over the years a tradition and a structure that would ensure consistent attention by competent managers to the day-to-day operations of departments and agencies', (Sundquist, 1995:398). At the sametime customer-centred model of change has been criticized for using the wrong metaphor. Frederickson (1994) argues that citizens are not customers of government rather they are its owners who elect leaders to represent their interests.

CONCLUSION

Administrative reform, as has been demonstrated throughout this chapter, is an important concept. Notwithstanding the differences of opinion pertaining to what it means and what kind of strategies need to be adopted for its implementation in diverse cultures, unanimity of views prevail as to its importance in redesigning outdated civil services and in bringing about efficiency and economy in the delivery of public services. It is widely recognized that there is very little alternative to administrative reform if one wishes to keep a civil service and its personnel in tune with changing time and needs of the clientele. Moreover, if policy makers are interested in organizational renewal, administrative reform can be an effective tool to do just that. Any change effort faces resistance of one kind or another and administrative reform is no exception to this trend. But such resistance can be overcome if timely and appropriate strategies are adopted and suitable and well- timed actions follow. The value of administrative reform can hardly be over-emphasized in view of its manifold practical application.

The emergence of three approaches as discussed earlier considerably broadened and enriched the concept of administrative reform. More importantly, administrative reform's appeal in spite of numerous set backs and dismal failures, as a tool kit to fix multifarious problems facing developed and developing nations, is still considerable.

REFERENCES

Abueva, J. V. (1970). "Administrative Reform and ulture", in Lee, H. B. and Samonte, A. G. eds. *Administrative Reforms in Asia*.Manila: *Eastern Regional Organization for Public Administration*, pp. 21-47.

Anisuzzaman, M. and Khan, M. M. (1980). "Administrative Reform: Problems of Definition and Defining Characteristics", *Politics Administration and Change* (PAC) 5 (2): 27-40.

Bjur, W. E. and Caiden, G. E. (1981). "Administrative Reform and Institutional Bureaucracies" in Khan, M. M. eds. *Administrative Refom: Theoretical Perspective*. Dhaka: Centre for Administrative Studies, pp. 107-133.

Caiden, G. E. (1969). *Administrative Reform*. Chicago: Aldine.

Caiden, G. E. (1979). "Implementation: The Achilles Heel of Administrative Reform" in Leemans, A. F. ed. *The Management of Change in Government*. The Hague: Martinus Nijhoff, pp. 145-174.

Caiden, G. E. (1985) "Administrative Reform: A Global Perspective", *Indian Journal of Public Administration* (IJPA) 31 (3): 459-471.

Caiden, G. E. (1988). "The Vitality of Administrative Reform", *International Review of Administrative Sciences* (IRAS) 54: 331-357.

Caiden, G. E. (1991). *Administrative Reform Comes of Age*. New York: Walter de Gruyter.

Citizen's Charter, The (1991). *Raising the Standard: Britain's Citizen's Charter and Public Service Reforms*. London: Foreign and Commonwealth Office.

Davenport, T.H. (1993). "Need Radical Innovation and Continuous Improvement? Integrate Process Reengineering and TQM", *Planning Review* 21(3): 6-12.

Davenport, T.H. and Short, J. E. (1990). "The New Industrial Engineering: Information Technology and Business Process Redesign", *Sloan Management Review* 31(4): 11-27.

Dey, B. K. (1971). "Administrative Reform: A Perspective Analysis", *IJPA* 17(3).

Dror, Y. (1976). "Strategies for Administrative Reform" in Leemans, A. F. ed. *The Management of Change in Government*. The Hague: Martinus Nijhoff, pp. 126-141.

Frederickson, H. G. (1994). "The Seven Principles of Total Quality Politics", *Public Administration Times* 17(1): 9.

Halachmi, A. (1995). "Re-engineering and Public Management: Some Issues and Consideration", *IRAS* 61(3): 329-341.

Hammer, M. (1990). "Reengineering Work: Don't Automate, Obliterate", *Harvard Business Review* (HBR) 68(4):104-112.

Hammer, M. and Champy, J. (1993). *Reengineering the Corporation*. New York: Harper Collins.

Khan, M. M. (1980). "Administrative Reform" in Khan, M. M. *Bureaucratic Self-Preservation: Failure of Major Administrative Reform Efforts in the Civil Service of Pakistan*. Dhaka: University of Dhaka pp. 52-70.

Kruger, P. D. (1990). "Reengineering : A Competitive Advantage", *Appliance Manufacturer* 41(4): 31-32.

Lee, H.B. (1970). "The Concept, Structure and Strategy of Administrative Reform: An Introduction" in Lee, H. B. and Samonte, A. G. eds. *Administrative Reforms in Asia*. Manila: Eastern Regional Organization for Public Administration.

Lee, H. B. (1976). "Bureaucratic Models and Administrative Reform" in Leemans, A. F. ed. *The Management of Change in Government*. The Hague: Martinus Nijhoff.

Leemans, A.F. (1976) ed. *The Management of Change in Government.* The Hague: Martinus Nijhoff.

Moe, R.C. (1994). "The 'Reinventing Government' Exercise: Misinterpreting Problem, Misjudging the Consequences", *Public Administration Review* (PAR) 54(2): 111-122.

Mottram, R. (1994). "Improving Public Services in the United Kingdom", paper presented in the Inaugural Conference of the Commonwealth Association of Public Administration and Management held in Charlottetown, Prince Edward Island, Canada from August 28 to August 31.

Mukarjee, N. K. (1971). "Formulation of Administrative Reform Strategies", in *Interregional Seminar on Major Administrative Reforms in Developing Countries.* Vol. 2: Technical Papers, New York: United Nations, pp. 45-54.

Nathan, R.P. (1995). "Reinventing Government: What Does It Mean?", *PAR* 55(2):213-215.

Nunberg, B. and Nellis, J. (1990). *Civil Service Reform and the World Bank*. Working Paper 422. Washington, D. C.: The World Bank.

Osborne, D. and Gaebler, T. (1992). *Reinventing Government: How the Entrepreneurial Spirit is Transforming the Public Sector. Reading*, MA: Addison-Welsey.

Pollitt, C. (1985). *Managerialism and the Public Services: The Anglo- American Experience*. London: Basil Blackwell.

Quah, J. S. T. (1981). "Administrative Reform: A Conceptual Analysis" in Khan, M. M. eds. *Administrative Reform: Theoretical Perspective.* Dhaka: Centre for Administrative Studies, pp. 32-67.

Saxena, A. P. (1980) ed. *Administrative Reforms for Decentralized Development.* Kuala Lumpur: Asian and Pacific Development Administration Centre.

Sundquist, J.L. (1995). "The Concept of Governmental Management: Or, What's Missing in the Government Report", *PAR* 55(4): 398-399.

United Nations (1979). *Handbook on the Improvement of Adminis-*

trative Management in Public Administration. New York: United Nations.

United Nations (1981). *Priority Areas for Action in Public Administration and Finance in the 1980s*. New York: United Nations.

United Nations (1982). *Changes and Trends in Public Administration and Finance for Development: Second Survey 1977-1979*. New York: United Nations.

United Nations (1983). *Enhancing Capabilities for Administrative Reform in Developing Countries*. New York: United Nations.

Wilenski, P. (1986). "Administrative Reform: General Principles and the Australian Experience", *Public Administration* (PA) 64: 257-276.

CHAPTER 2

Administrative Reforms in British India and United Pakistan

INTRODUCTION

Administrative reforms in the context of any country need to be understood in terms of past developments and experiences in the area of civil service. Past experience not only gives indications as to what are feasible within a given context but also what can be achieved with changes in time.

The civil service system in Bangladesh evolved over a long period of time. Indian sub- continent has been ruled by Hindu kings and Muslim emperors. The dynastic rule necessitated administrative systems which were geared mostly to achieving the goals of maintaining integrity of the country. The twin focus of maintaining law and order and collection of revenues lay at the core of the responsibilities of public servants.

The present chapter analyses civil service reform efforts which were undertaken from time to time in the Indian Civil Service (ICS) and the Civil Service of Pakistan (CSP). The rationale for focusing on the ICS and the CSP is due to the fact that the present civil service system in Bangladesh continues to be influenced by the elite civil service designed and operationalized by the British and continued with almost in an unchanged manner in Pakistan.

COLONIAL LEGACY

The roots of the administrative system in Bangladesh can be directly traced to the colonization by the British of the Indian subcontinent for nearly two centuries, i.e. 1757 to 1947. The civil service has been and continues to be influenced by the British imperial heritage. To understand the civil service system in today's India, Pakistan and Bangladesh one must be aware of the developments that took place during the British period, as in independent India and Pakistan the elite civil services, i.e., the Indian Administrative Service (IAS) and the Civil Service of Pakistan (CSP), were created on the model of the Indian Civil Service (ICS).

The British designed a highly centralized and elite administrative service, i.e., the ICS. The ICS was the most important instrument that Britain used to perpetuate its control over India (Woodruff, 1954). The ICS added to and strengthened the British desire to keep strict control over the native population and officials of other services (Griffiths, 1952:195). Naturally, the members of the ICS became disdainful of Indian politicians and remained aloof from the masses.

The ICS had all the trappings of an elite civil service. It was a highly centralized bureaucracy with provisions for entry only at the lowest level for a very small number of candidates, who had to qualify in highly competitive examinations which required not only academic excellence, acquired through attendance at top universities in England, and much later in India, but also the "right" kind of social background. The policy of reserving key policy-making and policy-implementing positions in the field, i.e. at district and divisional levels, and in the secretariat, both at the central and provincial governments, for the members of the ICS was in line with the overall British administrative strategy in India (Khan, 1980:71).

ADMINISTRATIVE REFORMS IN THE ICS

Administrative reforms were introduced in the ICS in a gradual and step-by-step manner. The major reforms which changed the nature and character of the ICS were the introduction of the competitive examination as a mode of entry to the service, provision of systematic training for its members and the Indianization of the service (Khan, 1980:81-88).

Open Competitive Examinations

The introduction of open competitive examinations was the culmination of efforts of the framers of a charter and members of a committee. The Charter Act of 1853 made it clear that all higher positions in the Covenanted Civil Service (CCS) (predecessor of the ICS) from now on should be filled by specifically-designed open competitive examinations. In 1892 the CCS was officially designated as the Indian Civil Service (Misra, 1977:93).

A Committee headed by Lord Macaulay was appointed to submit a detailed plan for the future recruitment of the East India Company's civil servants. The Macaulay report was submitted in 1854. The company agreed in principle with the Committee's recommendations and took immediate steps to implement them in right earnest. The first competitive examination was held in 1855. The impact of the Committee's report on the civil service was substantial. The open competition conditioned the ICS for nearly a hundred years (Giffiths, 1952:192).

Systematic Training

The need to train the company's servants was felt acutely and expressed forcefully by Lord Wellesley. Wellesley believed that to carry on their work in the judicial, revenue, political and financial departments, the company's servants needed a new range of skills in language and law in addition to a broad education to help them develop standards of judgment (Cohn, 1966:111). To remedy the situation, Wellesley established the Fort William College in 1800 without prior approval of the Court of Directors of the company. The programme of instruction was very comprehensive and ambitious. The trainees were to spend three years in the college learning oriental languages, classics and social science subjects. They were to be examined twice a year to evaluate their understanding and mastery of the subjects taught. Unfortunately, the Court of Directors did not agree with Wellesley's vision of broad-based training in India and instructed him in 1802 to confine the college curriculum only to oriental language instruction. The college continued to do exactly that till its abolition in 1854.

But Wellesley's idea was vindicated when the Court of Directors of the company in 1803 decided to set up a college in England to train the future European servants of the company in such subjects as classics, literature, mathematics, political economy, oriental languages, natural philosophy, laws of England, etc. Consequently, the East India College, popularly known as the Haileybury College, was established at Hartford in 1805 and shifted in 1809 to Haileybury (Misra, 1977:69). The college was abolished in 1853 as a result of the deliberations of the Macaulay Committee.

Though both the colleges had to be closed prematurely they had considerable impact on the ICS and its successors. First, Fort William College was first institution which provided comprehensive training to the company's servants. Second, by requiring that the company's personnel from the three presidencies of Bombay, Calcutta and Madras be trained together, it created an all-India character for the college as well as paved the way for centralized training of higher civil servants in independent Bangladesh, India and Pakistan. Third, the high standard of teaching at Haileybury College provided variety and diversity to broaden the mental horizon of the trainees.

INDIANIZATION

The issue of Indianization of the ICS had been a long-standing demand of the Indian leaders. The nature and extent of Indianization depended on the recommendations of various commissions appointed from time to time and the pressure exerted by Indian leaders. The demands included simultaneous holding of ICS examinations in both India and England and the raising of the age limits of the candidates for appearing in such examinations.

The Islington Commission, 1912-1915, in its report submitted in 1917 rejected the demand of simultaneous holding of ICS examinations in India but instead recommended that of all available positions in the ICS, 75 percent be recruited in England and the rest be filled from among Indians by nomination. Against the backdrop of hostile public opinion the British government decided to appoint one more commission and shelve the Islington Commission report. The Montagu-Chelmsford Report of 1918 suggested that 33 percent of the posts in the ICS should be recruited in India and that this should be increased by one and one-half percent annually. But the first concrete step for planned Indianization of the ICS had to wait till the government's acceptance of the Lee Commission Report. The Commission appointed in 1924 recommended that for all vacancies in the ICS, twenty percent should be filled by promotion from the provincial civil services (dominated by the Indians) and the remaining 80 percent be recruited directly from among Europeans and Indians in equal numbers. These recommendations were accepted by the government.

In 1922 for the first time the ICS examinations were held simultaneously in England and India. Also the Indian youths started going to England to study and take examinations there. The age limit for the examination was also raised. As a result of all these developments an increasing number of Indians began to enter the ICS.

The process of Indianization was a gradual one. It evolved over a long period of time. The degree and extent of Indianization were the resultant of the increasing political agitation and discontent among the Indians. But the "concessions" made in this regard from time to time were intended to appease selected sections of the Indian society. There had been considerable gap between policy pronouncements and their implementation regarding admission of Indians in the CCS and the ICS. The Imperial interest of the British Raj to a large extent dictated its policy towards Indianization (Khan, 1982:46).

PAKISTANI LEGACY

Pakistan at independence in 1947 inherited a well-developed bureaucratic system. At the core of this bureaucratic system was the Civil Service of Pakistan (CSP). The CSP was truly derivative in structure and ethos from the ICS (Bribanti, 1966:97). The CSP had been developed, influenced, and conditioned largely by its administrative heritage, which was unmistakably British. Its elitist character ensured its exclusive monopoly over key policy-making and policy-implementing positions in the realm of public service (Khan, 1979:134). Naturally, the CSP considered itself as the legitimate heir to the ICS of undivided India.

MAJOR ADMINISTRATIVE REFORM EFFORTS AND THE CSP

In Pakistan a number of commissions, committees and experts were appointed to study the public service and to recommend measures for improvements. Of these, five reports i.e., Egger, Gladieux, Cornelius '62, Power '69 and Cornelius '70 critically examined the existing administrative system and recommended far-reaching measures to overhaul the system. None of the reform bodies found justification for retaining an administrative system which had lost its usefulness and utility, and only encouraged the perpetuation of inequity and injustice in the recruitment, training, promotion, and pay among different civil services (Khan, 1980:128).

The recommendations of the above-mentioned five reform bodies ranged from the abólition of all-Pakistan services and their replacement with a single unified civil service; provision of lateral entry; giving comparable status to Heads of Departments and Secretaries of Ministries; raising the status of the Public Service Commission; and abolition of the Establishment Ministry (Kennedy, 1987:56-64).

None of the recommendations of the five bodies were accepted. During the existence of united Pakistan (1947-1971) no major reform was effectuated in the civil service system in general and in the CSP in particular. The resistance to major administrative reforms emanated from within and was sustained by the members of the CSP. The CSP felt threatened by the recommendations and organized effectively to block their acceptance. The outcome, from the CSP's point of view, was remarkable. Both the Egger and Gladieux reports were labeled secret and barred from public circulation for over a decade. "As an elitist group in Pakistan bureaucracy the CSP wield(ed) tremendous power and influence . . . it was able to prevent the publication of two reports (Egger and Gladieux) which were critical in their comments on its role and efficiency" (Sayeed, 1967:155-156). "He (Egger) perhaps considered too lightly that his recommendations directly threatened officials with status and power (CSP) in the administrative structure" (Gorvine, 1966:189). The opposition to the Pay and Services Commission, 1959-1962, popularly known as the First Cornelius Commission, was open, organized and well-orchestrated. The members of the CSP took a very active and leading role in waging a sustained campaign to block the efforts of the Commission. "As an organized and privileged group within the civil service system, the CSP had everything to lose because such proposals deeply threatened the elite status and exclusiveness of the CSP, particularly the attack (of the commission) on its privileged system of earmarked jobs" (Gorvine, 1966:202).

Two members of the Commission belonging to the CSP disagreed with the majority opinion and submitted a dissenting note justifying the maintenance of the status quo. The CSP National Association expressed its solidarity in public with its two senior dissonant colleagues. One member of the CSP even took to writing to support the continuation of the preeminent position of the CSP (Husain, 1967a; 1967b). The same fate befell the Report of the Working Group on the Reorganization of the Public Service Structure 1969, popularly known as the Power Report and Services Reorganization Committee Report, 1970, popularly known as the Second Cornelius Committee Report.

Besides CSP opposition, there was almost no political support for reform. This is understandable. After the assassination of the first Prime Minister of Pakistan in 1951, political instability and bureaucratic dominance of the statecraft became permanent feature of the governance system. The military was supportive of a political system which was headed and controlled by two non-elected chief executives in succession who happened to be senior civil servants. But in 1958 the military decided to formally take over power. The military rule lasted in one form or another till the dismemberment of Pakistan in December 1971.

CONCLUSION

Civil service systems in Bangladesh, India and Pakistan continue to be influenced in a significant manner by British colonial administrative practices and ethos even fifty years after the end of the British rule of the Indian subcontinent. The administrative systems in all the three countries still rest on centralization, elitism and distrust of both people and elected people's representatives.

The Indian Civil Service (ICS) designed by British as an instrument to rule a vast empire was retained with changed nomenclatures in all three countries long after their independence. Civil service reforms in united Pakistan, like in the British days, mostly concentrated on cosmetic changes rather than drastic overhauling which was recommended by a number of reform bodies. Weak political leadership, lack of political will and bureaucratic intransigence effectively combined to frustrate all efforts in united Pakistan to breakaway from an administrative system whose time had clearly passed.

REFERENCES

Bribanti, R. (1966). *Research on the Bureaucracy of Pakistan*. Durham, N. N.: Duke University Press.

Cohn, B. S. (1966). "Recruitment and Training of British Civil Servants in India", in Bribanti, R. ed. *Asian Bureaucratic Systems Emergent From the British Imperial Tradition*. Durham, N.C.: Duke University Press, pp. 87-140.

Gorvine, A. (1966). "Administrative Reform: Functions of Economic and Political Change" in Birkhead, G.S.ed. *Administrative Problems in Pakistan*. Syracuse, N.Y.: Syracuse University Press, pp. 185-211.

Griffiths, P. (1952). *The British Impact on India*. London : Macdonald.

Husain, I. (1969a). "An Analysis of the Assumptions Made in the Cornelius Report", *NIPA Journal* 10:90 - 100.

Husain, I. (1969b). "Conceptual Analysis of Civil Reform in Pakistan", *Administrative Science Review* 3: 64-76.

Kennedy, C.H. (1987). *Bureaucracy in Pakistan*. Karachi: Oxford University Press.

Khan, M. M. (1979). "Civil Service of Pakistan as an Institution : Reasons for Resistance to Change", *The Indian Political Science Review* 13(2): 133-153.

Khan, M. M. (1980). *Bureaucratic Self-Preservation : Failure of Major Administrative Reform Efforts in the Civil Service of Pakistan*. Dhaka: University of Dhaka.

Khan, M. M. (1982). "Indianization of the Covenanted Civil Service: A Constitutional Perspective", *PAC* 7(1): 40-47.

Misra, B. B. (1977). *The Bureaucracy in India: A Historical Analysis of Development up to 1947*. Delhi: Oxford University Press.

Sayeed, K. B. (1967). *The Political System of Pakistan*. Boston: Houghton Mifflin.

Woodruff, p. (1952). *The Men Who Ruled India: The Guardians*. London: Jonathan Cape.

CHAPTER 3

Bureaucratic Culture in Bangladesh

INTRODUCTION

Bureaucratic dominance of almost every aspect of human life is the hallmark of the present time. Bureaucracy, as a form of organization, is universally recognized as the most powerful tool designed to bring people together to perform a variety of tasks. For Weber 'in a modern state the actual ruler is necessarily and unavoidably the bureaucracy' (Weber, 1968:1393). This is so because 'one of the outstanding features of bureaucracy is that it tends to engulf and dominate an increasing number of social, economic and political activities' (Nachmias and Rosenbloom, 1980:14). Weber coined the term 'universal bureaucratization' to describe this process.

It has been argued that 'bureaucratic behaviour is substantially different as language and personality take on new meaning and forms in bureaucracy' (Nachmias and Rosenbloom, 1980:23). The difference between bureaucracy and other forms of social organization becomes clear if one looks at the norms of the former. The norms of a bureaucratic organization are 'precision, stability, stringency of discipline, reliability, calculability of results, formal rationality, formalistic impersonality and formal equality of treatment' (Hummel, 1977:9). 'Perhaps more than any other form of social organization, bureaucracy embodies the values of rationality and impersonality, that have come to dominate modern societies' (Meyer, 1972:1). Any organization in reality is a composite image of the attitudes, values and beliefs of its members, specially its top level officials (Gawthrop, 1969:11). Beside rationality and impersonality, culturally the other values which a bureaucrat care about are control and efficiency (Hummel, 1977:3).

This chapter does two things. First, it tries to clarify the concept of bureaucratic culture by distinguishing it from related concepts, i.e., organizational culture and administrative culture. Second, it explores selected dimensions of bureaucratic culture in Bangladesh. The present exploration is intended to focus on selected components of bureaucratic culture and their impact on society at large.

CONCEPTUAL FRAMEWORK

Bureaucracy has attracted the attention of scholars for a long time. Many social scientists have offered definitions of the concept and studied various dimensions of it. Albrow (1970: 84-105) has discussed, analyzed, organized and integrated seven competing concepts of bureaucracy. Following Albrow bureaucracy is considered in the context of this chapter as *rule by officials*. This perspective of bureaucracy is premised on the distribution of power in society and influence of officials in the governance process. The underlying implication of this way of looking at bureaucracy is that either officials assume political power or that within a representative system they are relatively dominant vis-a-vis other forces in society (Zafarullah, 1992:4).

Before embarking on a discussion of bureaucratic culture it is appropriate that one talks about culture in general along with other related terms like organizational culture and administrative culture. This needs to be done to provide a perspective of what follows so as to clarify meanings of terms which are similar in more than one ways.

Culture is the visible manifestation of the entire gamut of human endeavours. Still one needs to look for a definition of culture which is comprehensive yet meaningful. This is no easy task. After surveying more than hundred definitions of culture two scholars conclude that the best definition is the following: 'Culture consists of patterns, explicit and implicit, of and for behaviour acquired and transmitted by symbols, constituting the distinctive in artifacts' (Kroeber and Kluckhohn, 1952:181). The major characteristics of culture can be summed up like this: it is historical; including ideas, patterns and values; is selective, is learned; is based upon symbols; is an abstraction from behaviour; and is a product of behaviour (Kroeber and Kluckhohn, 1952:157).

Organizational culture is that set of beliefs and expectations shared by organization members which produce norms and shape behaviour. Behaviour takes the form of styles of action which typically reflect responses that have proven successful in the past.

Administrative culture is the set of values and understandings which influences the behaviour of organizations and the members of organizations (Peters, 1990:421). Administrative culture provides a general format within which the administration defines its tasks and the people respond to the attitude, behaviour, manner and the style of administrative functionaries (Thakur, 1990:481).

Administrative culture is the product of not only the people's cognitive, perceptive and evaluating orientations towards their administrative system, but also the entire gamut of traditional, societal, historical and cultural (including religious) values that influence as well as govern the bureaucracy's own behaviour and its professional norms, i.e. rationality, impersonality, technology and efficiency (Jain and Dwivedi, 1990 :436).

Nachmias and Rosenbloom (1978 :12-13) feel that orientations (cognitive, effective and evaluative) of both citizens and bureaucrats towards the bureaucracy are crucial for understanding bureaucratic culture. Two variables in bureaucratic organizations can be used to assess congruence in orientations. The variables are personnel and organizational dynamics. The relevant questions to be asked in understanding the personnel are: (a) whether bureaucrats form an elite; (b) whether they adequately represent significant social segments of the population; and (c) what is the public's image of bureaucrats personality, efficiency and character. Organizational dynamics, on the other hand, is to be viewed from two perspectives – administrative performance and political performance

-- within the framework of the bureaucratic structure. Administrative performance is to be examined in terms of orientations towards the treatment of clients, efficiency, the nature of bureaucratic processes (recruitment and promotion) and bureaupathologies. In assessing political performance such variables as political responsiveness, national development, social integration, provision of justice are contents of policy outputs.

Smith (1974) defines bureaucratic culture as 'the historical environment seen from within' and stresses bureaucrats' orientations towards (a) the political system and (b) political action. He points to the bureaucracy's tendency to become politically involved. Bureaucratic distinctiveness and involvement are two components of this tendency. The nature and extent of the political role of the bureaucracy can be understood by looking at two components together. .

Smith suggests that a bureaucracy has clear sub-system autonomy with the capability of adopting to and shaping its relevant environment. This provides bureaucracy with a distinctiveness which, in turn, is related to the cultural traits of the bureaucracy. The relationship between the political and bureaucratic cultures takes three forms. Firstly, because of dominance of the prevailing societal political culture it is impossible for bureaucracy to maintain sub-system autonomy. Secondly, as a result of sharp contradiction between the value patterns of the political elite and members of the bureaucracy an endemic conflict may develop between the two. One of the consequences of such a conflict might lead to estrangement of the higher civil servants from the political authorities. Finally, bureaucracy has an 'isolative' character and maintains a strong technical-managerial ethos.

It is difficult, if not outright impossible, to pinpoint differences in clear terms between organizational culture, administrative culture and bureaucratic culture. This becomes evident when one analyses the definitions provided in this section. Organizational culture would normally be expected to cover wider areas. But this does not appear to be the case. For Peters there is no difference between organizational culture and administrative culture. On the other hand, both Thakur and Dwivedi and Jain put administrative culture in a much broader canvass. Thakur mentions the role of people in shaping administrative culture while Dwivedi and Jain bring in a host of other factors like tradition, history and religion to discern the nature of administrative culture.

The discussion on bureaucratic culture has focused both on micro variables like personnel and organizational dynamics and macro variables like the political system and political action. But no clear-cut distinction can be maintained among micro and macro variables as both play important roles in developing and moulding bureaucratic culture.

Bureaucratic culture is rooted in history and traditions of a country. The esoteric traits a bureaucracy acquires and internalizes over the years reflects its natural evolution as an institution. External as well as internal environments of a bureaucracy shape the development of a peculiar bureaucratic culture that exhibit a bureaucracy's orientation towards itself and its environment.

Bureaucratic culture in this context means *patterns of behaviour that reflect the totality of certain distinctive values, assumptions, beliefs, sentiments and attitudes shared by members of a bureaucracy.*

BUREAUCRATIC CULTURE IN BANGLADESH

The inhabitants of the countries in South Asia are closely interrelated and their cultures reflect a unity in diversity. The unity can be explained in terms of the region's character of culture; the diversity can be viewed in terms of the physical features of the land and the people, the variety of regional languages, the political divisions, the differences in religious persuasions and the divergence of the food habit (Anisuzzaman 1979:5). The inheritance of common source explains the similarities of the cultural traits of Bangladesh which has always been pre-eminently rural and agricultural (Siddiqui 1982:67). Three major religions, i.e. Hinduism, Bhuddism and Islam have significantly influenced Bengali culture and shaped thought, behaviour, art and architecture of Bengali people. People have usually been not ambitious, easy going and non-militant as they lived peacefully in a land of plenty. But there have been significant changes in the life of Bengalis mainly due to the two hundred years of British rule of the Indian subcontinent. Still values, beliefs, rituals, arts and literature and popular entertainment reflect the pervasive influence of rural life.

The bureaucratic culture in Bangladesh has been moulded by both structural rigidities of an inherited colonial system of administration and the consequent behavioural patterns of bureaucrats. The behavioural patterns of bureaucrats have dramatically altered due to changed social, economic and political factors. All these have greatly influenced drastic changes in the values, norms, beliefs and perceptions of bureaucrats.

Some have viewed bureaucratic culture in Bangladesh in terms of dysfunctional aspects of bureaucratic behaviour believing these to be malleable to interventions designed to produce positive change. Accordingly, six general themes pertaining to bureaucratic behaviour in Bangladesh have been identified. These are: centralization of authority; multiple layers of decision making; a regulatory, rather than a facilitative, *modus operandi*, and a related systemic lack of trust; lack of adequate public accountability; lack of commitment; and lack of an incentive structure to encourage initiative and award excellence (Bretts et al., 1988: 97-98). Others have looked at bureaucratic culture in Bangladesh both in terms of systemic rigidities as well as behavioural dysfunction of those working within such systems. These are : excessive reliance on hierarchy; elaborate formal rules and procedures; excessive control; lack of trust in subordinates; diffusion of accountability through overlapping checks and balances; and a loss of accountability and control (Khan et al., 1989: 9).

Rahman and Cole (1992) also agree with the observations of Bretts et al. and Khan et al. (1989) in terms of the basic tenets of bureaucratic culture in Bangladesh. The difficulties involved in studying bureaucratic culture in any country is readily appreciated. The intention here is to analyze important components of bureaucratic culture in Bangladesh. The components have been identified by observing the behavioural patterns of a number of bureaucrats at different levels in the public bureaucracy.

The components of bureaucratic culture have been viewed below in terms of bureaucrats contact with citizens/clientele, their interaction with politicians in power and their dialogue with international donors and aid agencies.

CORRUPTION

Corruption is one of the most dominant components of bureaucratic culture in Bangladesh. Corruption has been institutionalized in the public service. No one denies the existence of large-scale corrupt practices perpetuated by bureaucrats any more. But there are differences of opinion in terms of nature, level and extent of corruption.

Corrupt practices in the domain of public service is not new. The civil servants during the Mughal period and East India Company's rule regularly accepted bribe from people. Many civil servants during the Pakistan period also engaged in various kinds of corruption.

Though corruption has been a part of bureaucratic culture for a long time, its tentacles have engulfed entire civil service only during last twenty-five years. The level of corruption varies depending on how influential a position the particular bureaucrat holds. The bureaucrats have by and large become accustomed to live a life style far beyond their legal income (Zafarullah, 1987). The citizens have accepted the stark reality that nothing moves without adequately "satisfying" the concerned bureaucrat. Wide-scale existence of corrupt practices have had two negative consequences. First, the delivery of services provided to the citizens has been affected. This is because there is a clear antipathy against critically analyzing government's functions; as a result, wastage, inefficiency and pilferage in the public sector abound (Report of the Task Force, 1991:221-222). Second, collection of revenue has been minimal. A recent study at the sub-national level provides clear indication of the extent of massive corruption perpetuated by civil servants at that level mostly in connivance with elected officials and its adverse impact on revenue collection (Rahman, 1994:339-358). Also information supplied by the Finance Division of the Ministry of Finance shows that over a period of twenty-two years, 1971-1993 taka 18,000 crore were lost in the public sector due to misappropriation of public funds and theft (Alam, 1996). But this amount which is substantial for a resource-poor and aid-dependent country is only the tip of the iceberg if one takes into consideration all cases of corruption that have been reported by the Bureau of Anti-Corruption over the years.

Almost all forms of corruption can be noticed among bureaucrats in Bangladesh. These include: abuse of authority, bribery, favouritism, extortion, fraud, patronage, theft, deceit, malfeasance and illegality (Caiden, 1991:492).

It may be an interesting exercise to discern what and why of such large-scale corruption. First, bureaucrats involved in corrupt practices in most cases do not lose their jobs. Very rarely they are dismissed from service on charges pertaining to corruption. Still rarely they are sent to prison for misusing public funds. They have never been compelled to return to the state their ill-gotten wealth. Second, the law-enforcing officials including police personnel are extremely corrupt. They are happy to share the booty with other corrupt bureaucrats. Third, the people have a tendency not only to tolerate corruption but to show respect to those bureaucrats who made fortune through dubious means. The underlying assumption is that it does not matter how one has acquired wealth as long as he has done so. Fourth, it is easier for a citizen to get quick service because he has already "paid" the bureaucrat rather than wait for his turn. In other words, there is now social acceptance of corruption by public officials. This is why, barring occasional public pronouncements, the representatives of the people are unwilling to take effective measures to curb corrupt practices in public dealings. Also many elected officials, including members of parliament and ministers, are known to be involved in large-scale corruption. The Director-General of the Bureau of Anti- Corruption and a senior civil servant known for his integrity and honesty was transferred to the Ministry of Education because he ordered a thorough probe against four ministers, scores of Members of Parliament (MPs) and a number of senior civil servants (*Daily Janakantha*, 10 May 1995). There have been numerous and repeated allegations of corruption against those individuals. It is widely believed that the Director- General of the Bureau of Anti-Corruption was suddenly transferred due to his crusade against corruption and his unwillingness to stop the probe. So it cannot be expected in the existing socio-politico-economic situation that bureaucratic and political elite will start a campaign against corruption in public life as it adversely affect their individual, group and coterie interests.

AUTHORITARIANISM

Authoritarianism is part and parcel of Bengali culture. Overwhelming majority of the population are Muslims. Islam, the religion of the Muslims, directs its adherents to bestow faith in one God, one Prophet and one holy book -- the Koran. In the family all authority is vested with the father. He lays down the rules for others to follow. The children from early ages are taught to respect elders and accept their authority without questioning the basis of such authority.

There is still considerable emphasis on age and seniority in appointment and promotion within the public service system. In the process merit is underemphasized. One of the consequences of seniority is concentration of power at the top of the hierarchy and delay in giving decisions on important matters. Red tapism is a regular phenomenon in Bangladesh public service. Communication flows usually downward. Rarely subordinates can give meaningful feedback to superiors. To keep the superiors in good humour and to facilitate their career path many subordinates indulge in sycophancy. This adversely affects development and maintenance of healthy working relation between officials at different levels in the hierarchy and encourages and perpetuates authoritarian tendencies within public sector.

CENTRALIZATION OF AUTHORITY

The tendency to concentrate power at the top of the hierarchy in fewer officials is a legacy from the colonial past. The British, as an imperial power, needed hierarchy to ensure control over vast native population in India. In the early 1920s there was one British civilian officer for 86,000 Indians. This meant that about 3,500 British civilian officers serving in all departments had control over 300 million Indians. These officers were ably supported by 944 Indian civilian officers. Such control was premised on lack of trust of the Indian population by those who were at the helm of administration. Consequently, rules and regulations emphasized hierarchy and downward communication.

The situation did not change after independence in 1947 and the emergence of two sovereign states -- India and Pakistan. In Pakistan, closely following the British practice, the bureaucratic system had been organized around four closely related factors, i.e. the secretariat system, the systematic preference for generalists, the cadre system of organization and rigid and formal patterns of rank hierarchy (Kennedy, 1987:1).

In Bangladesh all the four factors are not only present in the civil service system but they significantly mould behaviours and ethos of civil servants.

All policy making powers continue to be concentrated at the secretariat. The official work manual, i.e., the Rules of Business till recently gave considerable power to the secretary. He still remains the chief advisor to the minister on policy making; acts as the financial head of the ministry; and assumes the role of sole custodian of relevant information on which policies are based. Consequently, secretaries most of whom are generalists, exercise a great deal of power and influence in governmental decision making. The last government of Khaleda Zia failed to change the Rules of Business even after five years in power. The present government under the leadership of Sheikh Hasina has already initiated a number of actions to ensure political control of the bureaucracy.

ELITISM

Elitism is pervasive within the civil service system in Bangladesh. Elitism is a direct legacy from the days of the British Raj. This is reflected in how different services have been organized within the civil service system and how civil servants interact with citizens.

The British devised an administrative system which was premised on elitism and centralization of authority. All powers were vested with a select band of civil servants who were chosen through competitive examinations and were destined to occupy key positions at a relatively younger age with supervisory responsibilities over all other governmental functionaries. Thus gap between the ICS, i.e. the members of the elite service and the non-ICS was reinforced by a cultural and social gap (Heginbotham, 1975:41). It has been argued that these generalists who even administered special departments, not because they possessed specialized knowledge, but because they could, by virtue of superior qualities of mind, training and experience had a better grasp of organizational and administrative problems (Mishra, 1977:392).

The elitism which moulded the civil service system in the united Pakistan between 1947 and 1971 and resisted development of professionalism on the basis of expert knowledge therein is very much evident even in today's Bangladesh civil service. The system among other things indicates strong influence of elitism in the way the civil service is organized and managed.

The preference for the generalists is reflected in three ways: (i) in recruitment, (ii) pre-eminence enjoyed by generalist cadres within the civil service, and (iii) closed career concept.

At the time of recruitment in the civil service all subjects in the examinations are considered to have equal value and consequently no preference is given for relevance. Members of the generalist cadre, i.e. Bangladesh Civil Service (Administration), occupies a relatively privileged position within the civil service in terms of promotion, transfer, posting and training abroad. This situation, similar to that of today's Pakistan, creates enormous problems for those who belong to specialist and functional cadres in Bangladesh and attempt to enter the power elite encounter two formidable hurdles (Kennedy, 1987). First, they must demonstrate extraordinary personal competence to overcome the widely-held belief that technocrats are poor administrators. Second, they must also overcome norms and practices designed to favour generalists. The civil service in Bangladesh is still a 'closed shop' like in the past. Everyone has to start his or her career at the bottom of the hierarchy leaving almost no opportunity to enter laterally at the mid- or top- level. This practice has denied the civil service to utilize expertise and experience of professionals who are outside the domain of the civil service and has also encouraged in-breeding of mediocrity within.

LACK OF TRANSPARENCY

The tendency to mark everything secret and keeping citizens in the dark about decisions taken by the civil servants was in conformity with the viceregal system that British introduced in India. The administration was designed to serve only the imperial interest. So the issues of transparency in governmental activities and decisions were neither relevant nor important in that particular context.

The decision making process in the civil service in Bangladesh is still non-transparent. Interested citizens do not have any opportunity to learn about how particular decisions have been arrived at. Non-transparent decision making process has made it difficult to hold civil servants accountable for their decisions.

LACK OF ACCOUNTABILITY

The civil servants in British India were accountable to their immediate superiors. So bureaucratic accountability within the confines of the civil service was evident. But the missing components were the mechanisms, the ways and means and systems to ensure bureaucrats accountability to politicians. This was also not feasible as civil servants working in different states even under dyarchy (dual system) were made accountable for their actions to their superiors and through them to the Viceroy in Delhi who was the British monarch's representative in India. The British India was essentially an administrative state where civil servants, especially those belonging to the ICS, had more power, greater authority and higher status compared to elected politicians at different levels. Hence politicians even while holding ministerial berths had no control over civil servants working within their ministries.

Holding civil servants accountable for their actions has proved to be a difficult task in Bangladesh. Traditional mechanisms like hierarchy and supervision have mostly failed. Other mechanisms like parliamentary control through various committees and sub-committees, judicial intervention and press have largely been unsuccessful in making civil servants accountable for their acts of omission and commission. More significantly, ministerial control over senior civil servants is still in a flux as appropriate changes in relevant rules and regulations had not been seriously pursued by the Khaleda Zia government. This was strange catpulation of elected peoples representatives to powerful civil servants.

Citizens Treated as Children

This practice reflected a wide gap that existed between the rulers and the ruled in British India. The civil servants as part of the ruling eilte were indoctrinated to keep as little direct contact with ordinary people as possible. This was a deliberate move to create the image of British civilian officers as superior beings who could perform their assigned roles efficiently and justly. The civil servants were expected to make all decisions as they had power and authority of the cadre behind them. Hence the practice of excessive dependence of the population on the civil servants developed and the resultant assumption of guardianship role by the civil servants at the field level was accepted.

The tendency to treat citizens as minors by civil servants have not changed with independence. Rather the entire edifice of the administration has been built in a way as to encourage perpetual dependence of citizens on civil servants. This development has adversely affected the self-esteem of the citizens and discouraged citizen participation and involvement in governmental affairs.

Resistance to Change

Bureaucrats in Bangladesh, especially those at the higher level, have been remarkably successful in thwarting each and every major effort to reform the public service system (Khan, 1991). Overhauling and recasting of the public service is a necessity as it continues to be afflicted by such bureaupathologies as 'alienation, arbitrariness, inaccessibility, inaction, indecision, inertia, indifference, ineffectiveness, insensitivity and irregularity' (Caiden, 1991:492).

These bureaupathologies have had several negative consequences. First, the bureaucrats have become increasingly inefficient and incompetent. Many of them are totally ignorant of the rules and regulations which are supposed to govern their conduct. At the same time, they talk of rules while denying genuine request for action from citizens. Sometimes lack of action on the part of the bureaucrats are justified on frivolous grounds.

Second, most of them show no initiative at all and lack vision for future. They mostly suffer from tunnel vision. They are preoccupied with the present and not concerned about the future. They are reactive by nature and not interested to be proactive even when situation so demands.

Third, most bureaucrats are discourteous in their dealing with ordinary people. Obviously, this is the result of a feeling of superiority on the part of the bureaucrats compared to the poor people. Bureaucrats usually harbour an overbearing attitude towards people-at large. The concept of service to the people is alien to them. The bureaucrats want to command the people. They feel it is their god given right. This results in harassment of the poor and powerless mostly in the hands of street-level bureaucrats. Laws, rules and regulations are interpreted and implemented in such a way that on many occasions the poor do not receive their due from the bureaucrats. On the other hand, bureaucrats irrespective of levels, are eager and interested to serve and fraternize with the rich and powerful segments of the population. The rich includes political, business, military and bureaucratic elites. Laws are interpreted either liberally or altogether ignored to give benefit to the power-holders in the society.

Fourth, the common people have a tendency to avoid contact with bureaucrats belonging to law-enforcing agencies and magistracy. The tendency is to rely on middleman to act as a go between the two parties. This always turns out to be very costly deal for the poor and lower middle class people as they are supposed to pay not only the concerned bureaucrat but also the middleman.

Fifth, bureaucrats in Bangladesh appear to be accountable to none. The internal mechanisms premised on hierarchy is rarely utilized. The external mechanisms,i.e. role of parliamentary committees and control by ministers have not been effective. In some cases, bureaucrats have been transferred or retired only after completion of their mandatory service period. Political victimization of bureaucrats sometimes have been taken the place of political control. This has had a negative impact on the morale of bureaucrats in general. Though the institution of ombudsman has been incorporated in the constitution of the country it has not yet been instituted in practice.

Finally, political rulers – both the elected representatives of the people and military personnel who usurped state power – found it convenient to tinker with the civil service system. In both cases political will to reform had been absent. The lack of commitment of political leadership to change can be explained in terms of benefits obtained by them in retaining the status quo. Political leaders in power have always depended heavily on the civil servants to govern. The civil servants, specially the senior ones, have found it convenient to enthusiastically serve those political masters who understood their arguments against change. Top-level bureaucrats have been and continue to be, in many cases, much more closer to the power centre i.e. the prime minister than many ministers and most members of parliament.

CONCLUSION

Bureaucratic culture in Bangladesh is both complex and multi-faceted. Many factors have contributed to its development and sustenance. But it has been increasingly realized that the existing bureaucratic culture is anti-people and oppressive in nature. Rajiv Gandhi, the late Indian Prime Minister, in a perceptive speech in December, 1985 summed up neatly the state of bureaucratic culture in India. Gandhi's description is equally applicable to Bangladesh. We have government servants who do not serve but oppress the poor and the helpless . . . who do not uphold the law . . . but connive with those who cheat the state, whole legions whose only concern is their private welfare at the cost of society. They have no work ethic, no feeling for the public cause, no involvement in the future of the nation, no comprehension of national goals, no commitment to the values of modern India. They have only a grasping mercenary outlook, devoid of competence, integrity and commitment (quoted in Arora, 1990:572-573).

Due to the prevailing bureaucratic culture public service has become synonymous with corruption, waste and inefficiency. The citizens have to pay more for poor service. This is because all the ingredients of a professional civil service are either totally or partially lacking in the bureaucratic culture of Bangladesh. These are: merit principle, guaranteed financial probity, respect for political neutrality, impartiality under law, commitment to serve any government well and accountable at all levels (Stowe, 1992:391).

REFERENCE

Alam, M.S (1996). "Corruption in Administration" (in Bangla), *Bangla Bazar Patrika* (a vernacular daily news paper) January 28, and 30.

Albrow, M. (1970). *Bureaucracy*. New York: Praeger.

Anisuzzaman (1979). *Social Aspects of Endogenous Intellectual Activity*. Tokyo: The United Nations University.

Arora, H.C. (1990). "Indian Administrative Culture and Bureaucracy", *IJPA* 36 (3): 567-576.

Bretts, R.H. et al. (1988). *The Utilization of Project Aid in Bangladesh: Findings and Recommendation: Final Report*. Vol. 1. Washington, D.C: Development Alternatives Incorporated.

Caiden, G.E. (1991). "What Really is Public Maladministration?", *PAR* 51 (6): 486-493.

Gawthrop, L.C. (1969). *Bureaucratic Behaviour in the Executive Branch*. New York: The Free Press.

Heginbotham, S.J. (1975). *Cultures in Conflict: The Four Faces of Indian Bureaucracy*. New York: Columbia University Press.

Hummel, R P. (1977). *The Bureaucratic Experience*. New York: St. Martin's Press.

Jain, R.B. and Dwivedi, O. P. (1990). "Administrative Culture and Bureaucratic Values in India", *IJPA* 36 (3): 435 - 450.

Janakantha, The (1995) (vernacular daily news paper) May 10.

Kennedy, C.H. (1987). *Bureaucracy in Pakistan*. Karachi: Oxford University Press.

Khan, M.M. (1980). *Bureaucratic Self Preservation: Failure of Major Administrative Reform Efforts in the Civil Service of Pakistan*. Dhaka: University of Dhaka.

Khan, M.M. (1991). *Politics of Administrative Reforms: A Case Study of Bangladesh*. Delhi: Ashish Publishing House.

Khan, M.M. et al. (1989). *Report of the Public Administration Efficiency Study: Main Report* Vol. 1. Washington, D.C.: Checci & Company.

Kroeber, A.L. and Kluckohn, C. (1952). "Culture: A Critical Review of Concepts and Definitions" in *Papers of the Peabody Museum* 47 (1), Cambridge, MA: Harvard University.

Mathur, K. (1991). "Bureaucracy in India: Development and Pursuit of Self Interest", *IJPA* 37 (4): 637 - 648.

Meyer, M.W. (19720. *Bureaucratic Structure and Authority*. New York: Harper and Row.

Mishra, B.B. (1977). *The Bureaucracy in India: A Historical Analysis of Development upto 1947*. Delhi: Oxford University Press.

Nachmias, D. and Rosenbloom, D.H. (1978). *Bureaucratic Culture*. New York: St. Martin's Press.

Nachmias, D. and Rosenbloom, D.H. (1980). *Bureaucratic Government USA*. New York: St. Martin's Press.

Peters, B.G. (1990). "Administrative Culture and Analysis of Public Organizations", *IJPA* 36 (3): 420-428.

Rahman, A.T.R. and Cole, J.M. (1992). *Public Administration Sector Study in Bangladesh: Formulation Mission Report*. New York: Public Administration Branch, United Nations Department of Economic and Social Development.

Rahman, M.H. (1994). "Decentralization and Rural Society in Bangladesh: A Study of Bureaucratic Constraints on Access". Unpublished Ph. D. Thesis. Submitted to the University of Wales, Swansea.

Siddiqui, A.R. (1982). *Literature of Bangladesh and Other Essays*. Dhaka: Bangladesh Book International.

Smith, G. (1974). "A Model of the Bureaucratic Culture", *Political Studies* 22:31-43.

Stowe, K. (1992). "Good Piano Won't Play Bad Music: Administrative Reform and Good Governance", *PA* 70 (Autumn): 387-394.

Task Forces (1991). "Development Administration" in *Report of the Task Forces on Bangladesh's Development Strategies for the 1990s*. Dhaka: University Press Limited.

Thakur, R.N. (1990). "Contemporary Administrative Culture and Indian Social Reality: Towards a Model-Building", *IJPA* 36 (3): 480-490.

Weber, M. (1968). *Economy and Society: An Outline of Interpretive Sociology*. 3 Vols. ed. G. Roth and C. Wittich, trans, E. Fischoff, et. al. N.Y. : Bedminister Press.

Zafarullah, H.M. (1987). "Public Administration in the First Decade of Bangladesh: Some Observations on Development and Trends", *Asian Survey* 27:459-476.

Zafarullah, H.M. (1992). *Understanding Bureaucracy: A Primer*. Dhaka: Academic Publishers.

CHAPTER 4

Civil Service in Bangladesh

INTRODUCTION

Any discussion of reforms must precede analysis of the object of such reforms. This chapter includes discussion on selected yet important aspects of civil service in Bangladesh. The two preceding chapters have already provided the context on which the discussion that follows is based.

This chapter describes the structure of and includes a profile of the civil service; discusses how the civil service is managed focusing on some of the vital areas; analyses key issues facing women in the civil service and includes an assessment as to the appropriateness of the size and relevance of the civil service in the present context.

STRUCTURE OF THE CIVIL SERVICE

In this section a description of the structure of the civil service is given. Also an attempt is made to explain various layers of government, i.e. central, district and thana (police station) including the central secretariat and its departments and agencies.

The administrative structure of the government consists of line and staff agencies both at the national and local levels. A large number of ministries constitutes the central secretariat. Each ministry consists of one or more divisions, i.e. whose numbers now stand at 35. Given the ever-changing shape of government, and the realignment of ministerial jurisdictions and transfer of functions, it is hazardous to categorize ministries, but they can be classified as three types : economic, including Ministries of Finance, Planning and Commerce; development, including Education, Health, Road & Road Transport Ministries; and service-oriented or welfare, including Ministries of Relief, Social Welfare, Labour and Manpower (World Bank, 1996a: 149) Public bodies operate under the administrative jurisdiction of relevant ministries. Baside ministries, there are 50 divisions, 221 departments, 131 directorates and autonomous bodies and 153 state-owned enterprises (World Bank, 1996a: 1). A ministry and each of its constituent divisions formulate government policies within its predetermined boundaries. It is also involved in both supervising and reviewing the execution of its policies. Departments and directorates give executive direction in the implementation of policies of the ministry/division to which they are attached. Autonomous, semi-autonomous and state-owned enterprises perform specialized public functions or implement specific development tasks.

At the sub-national level, the structure of public administration extends through three tiers; division, district and thana. All these tiers are run and managed by civil servants. The divisional administration guides and supervises the activities of district administrative units under its jurisdiction. Coordination of developmental activities and deciding upon questions of revenue administration continues to be the cornerstone of local administration. Its crucial role encompasses a wide-range of activities: land revenue administration, correctional services and development administration. But in recent years increasing conflict among the generalist officer, i.e. deputy commissioner and other technical civil servants, i.e. engineers, doctors, agriculturists posted at the district has created serious problems of coordination at that level. The thana is the lowest tier of field administration. Officers posted at that level perform regulatory as well as developmental functions.

A distinctive aspect of the civil service structure is organization of civil servants into semi-functional cadres. Subsequent to the completion of the selection process, direct recruits are assigned to an occupational cadre on the basis of performance, vacancies and preference of candidates. Usually, a civil servant remains a member of his originally chosen/assigned cadre throughout his/her career. His/her promotional prospect, job type and duties are determined to a large extent by association with his/her cadre.

The cadre system as it exists today reflects the vertical classificatory schema in operation. There are 29 cadres in the Bangladesh Civil Service (BCS). Among the BCS cadres at least three major types of services are noticed. These are : (i) generalist-administrative services which include BCS (Administration) and BCS (Food); (ii) functional services which include such services as BCS (Audit and Accounts), BCS (Customs and Excise) and BCS (Taxation); and (iii) specialist service which include such services as BCS (Fisheries), BCS (Public Works) and BCS (Technical Education). The structure of civil service also shows a rigid pattern of rank which corresponds to occupational type and hence the horizontal classification is based on a number of factors including levels of responsibility, educational requirements and pay range. Those who belong to classes II, III and IV are 'scheduled castes' in the civil service hierarchy. Most of them are condemned to stay in their designed classes throughout their working lives with only few are able to break the class barrier and move into next higher class.

PROFILE OF THE CIVIL SERVICE

In this section, a profile of the civil service is presented mostly concentrating on the size of the civil service. Also the size of the civil service in Bangladesh in relation to population is compared to situation obtaining in other developing countries. There are now 0.94 million people working in the civil service in Bangladesh (see Table 4.1). These individuals are in place in ministries/divisions, departments/directorates and autonomous bodies/corporations. On the other hand, the current strength of all 29 BCS cadres together stands at 34,848 (see Table 4.2). Analy-

Table 4.1 Class-wise strength of civil servants (as on 1 January 1992).

Class	MIN/DIV SANC	MIN/DIV EXIST	MIN/DIV VACANT	DEPT/DTE SANC	DEPT/DTE EXIST	DEPT/DTE VACANT	AUTO/CORP SANC	AUTO/CORP EXIST	AUTO/CORP VACANT	TOTAL SANC	TOTAL EXIST	TOTAL VACANT
(1)	(2)	(3)	(4)	(5)	(6)	(7)	(8)	(9)	(10)	(11)	(12)	(13)
Class-I	2128	1875	253	41951	32922	9029	50052	43888	644	94131	78685	15446
Class II	67	51	16	12670	10741	1929	29779	26066	3713	42516	5658	5658
Class III	4548	4132	416	482413	442859	39554	157169	132851	24318	644130	579842	6428
Class IV	2426	2343	83	175378	162819	12559	96927	86202	10725	274731	251364	23367
Total	9196	8401	768	712412	649341	63071	333927	289007	44920	1055508	946749	108759

SOURCE: Ministry of Establishment, Statistics of Civil Officers and Staff of GOPRB, Dhaka, 1992

Explanations: MIN = Ministries; DIV = Divisions; DEPT = Departments; DTE = Directorates; AUTO = Autonomous Bodies; CORP = Corporations; SANC = Sanctioned; EXIST = Existing sis of these two tables together provide a number of interesting facts.

Table 4.2. List of 29 BCS cadres and their cadre strength.

Cadre	Strength
Administration	6004
Agriculture	2009
Ansar	227
Audit and Accounts	280
Cooperative	149
Customs and Excise	143
Economic	531
Family Planning	322
Fisheries	659
Food	219
Foreign Affairs	230
Forest	159
General Educates	8510
Health	8313
Information	581
Judicial	626
Livestock	1479
Police	769
Postal	159
Public and Health Engineering	196
Public Works	631
Railway Transportation& Commercial	61
Roads & Highways	544
Statistical	107
Taxation	358
Technical Eucation	762
Tele-communication	476
Trade	476
Total	34,848

SOURCE: Discussion with officials in various ministries and members of cadres, 1994.

Table 4.3. Year-wise increase/decrease of civil officers and staff of the Government of Bangladesh (%).

Year	Class I	Class II	Class III	Class IV
1971	–	–	–	–
1977	51.46	–23.20	47.78	–58.92
1980	34.35	201.85	–5.37	121.17
1987	182.91	23.30	54.89	60.24
1988	13.83	3.65	10.29	–17.25
1989	–1.21	0.55	14.61	39.18
1990	4.34	–2.02	1.81	1.11
1991	0.93	0.87	0.85	2.00
1992	3.70	1.61	12.59	–21.64

SOURCE: Establishment Division, Statistics on Civil Employees of the Government of the People's Republic of Bangladesh, Dhaka, 1975.

Establishment Division, Statistics on Civil Employees of the GPRB,Dhaka, 1977.

Establishment Division, Statistics on Civil Employees of the GPRB, Dhaka, 1980.

Establishment Division, Statistics on Civil Employees of the GPRB, Dhaka, 1987.

Establishment Division, Statistics of Civil Officers and Staff of the GPRB, Dhaka, 1988.

Establishment Division, Statistics of Civil Officers and Staff of the GPRB, Dhaka, 1989.

Establishment Division, Statistics of Civil Officers and Staff of the GPRB, Dhaka, 1991.

Establishment Division, Statistics of Civil Officers and Staff of the GPRB, Dhaka, 1991.

First, the encadred officers account for only 3.68% of the total number of officers and employees working in the public sector. Second, officers of all cadres put together are less than half the size of actual number, i.e. 78,685 of class 1 officers. All cadre officers are class 1 civil servants but not all class 1 officers belong to cadres. This means that 43,837 non-cadre civil servants neither have the prospect of upward mobility nor vertical movement probability compared to their cadre colleagues who belong to the same class as they do. Third, one often hears the statement about top heavy administration when reference is made to the civil service. This implies that too many individuals are occupying positions at the top compared to those who are at the bottom. But the situation obtaining in reality is strikingly different. Of the total number of civil servants the percentage in terms of share of different classes is: class I 8.31%, class II 3.89%, class III 61.25% and class IV 26.55%. Taken together, classes III and IV employees constitute overwhelming majority of the total number of public sector personnel, i.e. 78.80%. Fourth, year-wise increase and decrease of civil servants of all categories has been shown in a compact manner (see Table 4.3) and in a rather detail manner (see Table 4.4) taking 1971 as the base year. These two tables indicate that significant increases in the number of civil servants occurred occasionally but not regularly. The huge increase in the numbers of class I, II and IV officers and employees can be explained in terms of the lapse of considerable period of time, i.e. seven years between 1980 and 1987 and the introduction of the upazila (sub-district) system between 1982-1983 which necessitated recruitment of a rather large number of public servants within a short span of time. Also decrease in the number of civil servants belonging to classes I and II and rather significant decrease for class IV indicated Khaleda Zia government's intention to keep the size of the civil service within reasonable bound.

Table 4.4 Year-wise changes in number of public servants.

Year	No	Change (%)
	Class I Staff of the GOB	
1971	11130	–
1977	16857	51.46
1980	22648	34.35
1987	64073	182.91
1989	72050	–1.21
1990	75180	4.34
1991	75877	0.93
1992	78685	3.70

Year	No	Change (%)
	Class II Staff of the GOB	
1971	12320	–
1977	9462	–23.20
1980	28561	201.85
1987	35216	23.30
1988	36501	3.65
1989	36703	0.55
1990	35960	–2.02
1991	36273	0.87
1992	36858	1.61
	Class III Staff of the GOB	
1971	245500	–
1977	362811	47.78
1980	343319	–5.37
1987	531762	54.89
1988	586455	10.29
1989	500792	–14.61
1990	509857	1.81
1991	514189	0.85
1992	578942	12.59
	Class I Staff of the GOB	
1971	185500	–
1977	76200	–58.92
1980	168530	121.17
1987	270054	60.24
1988	223475	–17.25
1989	3111036	39.18
1990	314480	1.11
1991	320768	2.00
1992	251364	–21.64

SOURCE: Same as Table 4.3

Fifth, it can be seen (Table 4.1) that compared to civil servants working at different levels in ministries/divisions the number of civil servants employed in directorates and autonomous bodies/corporations are much larger. This may be explained by the nature of work and the way individuals are recruited. Sixth, it becomes clear (from Table 4.3) that certain cadres like BCS (Administration), BCS (Health) and BCS (General Education) have huge number of members compared to other cadres. Seventh, the issue of size of a civil service is also invariably linked to the cost of maintaining such a service. Cost-effectiveness, therefore, becomes critical for a poor country like Bangladesh. It has been found that salaries of civil servants (including both officials and employees) and allowances and honorarium paid to them was 29.80% and 27.84% of the revenue budget for the financial years 1993-94 and 1994-95 respectively. This means that more than one-quarter of the revenue budget is spent on maintaining public sector work force. But this cost figure will significantly increase if one considers the fact that in two of the largest public sector areas, i.e. education and health, personnel expenditure is separately shown on the development budget. Also if one looks at the expenditure on civil service in terms of GDP then also the picture indicates that a much larger amount of money is spent on maintaining civil servants of all categories. Finally, it would be interesting to compare how many officials belonging to different cadres have been posted in the capital city, i.e. Dhaka and how many are working in districts and thanas. This figure would have indicated how close civil servants are vis-a-vis the clientele. Unfortunately, the Ministry of Establishment (MOE) does not have this kind of data. When contacted by the author the concerned senior official at MOE stated that despite repeated requests ministries and divisions did not furnish to the MOE exact number of their officials deployed at various field levels, i.e. divisions, districts and thanas.

The size of the civil service becomes an issue of great significance for an impoverished country like Bangladesh if it is perceived to be too big. Bigness or smallness is a relative matter. One of the ways of resolving it is to look at the situation in other developing countries. Compared to a number of developing countries and in relation to the total population of the country the size of the civil service is relatively small. The respective ratios of public employees to population are: Bangladesh 1.3%, Pakistan 2.2%, Ghana 2.3%, Chile 2.5%, Sri Lanka 5%, Argentina 6.4%, Uruguay 8.7%.

MANAGEMENT OF THE CIVIL SERVICE

The management of the civil service is still conducted within a more or less unified framework. The Ministry of Establishment (MOE) acts as the central personnel agency of the government of Bangladesh. It lays down the broad policies, principles and regulations for managing the civil bureaucracy and initiates measures for employee welfare and for improvement of procedures and techniques relating to personnel administration (Ahmed and Khan, 1990:28). It is also responsible for initial recruitment to all the cadre services and for disciplinary action and welfare in respect of all senior officials in the secretariat and outside (Ahmed, 1985:47-48). Though MOE has an overall responsibility for all major personnel matters and for overseeing their implementation by other ministries/divisions, its jurisdiction in routine day-to-day management of civil service has some limitations. At present, MOE manages directly only one cadre, i.e. BCS (Administration) out of 29 cadres. The other 28 cadres are controlled by their respective ministries/divisions. But rules and regulations governing civil servants are prepared by the MOE. Beside MOE plays key roles in such personnel areas as training, placement, transfer, promotion and discipline.

The other agency which performs important personnel functions pertaining to the civil service is the Bangladesh Public Service Commission (BPSC). The BPSC is a constitutional body. Its basic functions have been clearly spelled out in article 40 of the constitution of Bangladesh. The functions are (a) to conduct tests and examinations for the selection of suitable persons for appointment to the civil service of Bangladesh; (b) to advise the President on any service matter on which PSC is consulted under clause (2) of article 140 or on any matter connected with its functions which is referred to the PSC by the President; and (c) to perform such other functions as prescribed by law (Ahmed, 1990: 147).

But in reality the functional jurisdiction of BPSC now covers only gazatted class I and II officers belonging to strictly government organizations. The role of the BPSC has been circumscribed in the area of recruitment of civil servants by issuance of rules, regulations and ordinances by governments in the past (Khan, 1994). The BPSC Consultation Regulation of 1979 has taken away a large number of class I and class II posts from the purview of the BPSC. Also successive governments and authorities in the executive branch have willfully ignored the advice and suggestions of the BPSC in the areas of appointment, regularization and promotion of civil servants. In the past, on many occasions, the MOE deliberately tried to influence and obstruct the activities of the BPSC. This has been primarily due to the preeminent position of the MOE in the public service management in Bangladesh and relegation of BPSC to a subordinate agency of the former in the form of an attached department. This situation changed somewhat in 1989 when BPSC was accorded secretariat status and placed as a separate secretarial division in the president's secretariat. The BPSC is now a secretariat in the MOE. It is not surprising that BPSC still suffers from lack of qualified and trained personnel, shortage of office space and dearth of modern testing equipment. But the greatest danger that BPSC faced was the tendency of the last government to politicize it. The BNP government of Khaleda Zia made it a practice to appoint chairman and members of BPSC from among her political supporters and henchmen who lacked appropriate background, qualifications, knowledge, aptitude and thereby tarnishing the image and credibility of BPSC as a constitutional body.

AREAS IN CIVIL SERVICE MANAGEMENT

THE CADRE SYSTEM

The cadre system is enmeshed in controversies. It is under attack from professional civil servants of all shades. The number of its defenders are not many. They belong almost exclusively to the generalist cadres and more specifically, to the BCS (Administration) cadre.

In the cadre system every post is borne clearly against one or another cadre and no member of a particular cadre is expected to be posted in the post borne against another cadre. This implies that a civil servant who becomes a member of a particular cadre is clearly aware about his own lines and prospect for promotion.

But the bone of contention begins there. The seed of inter-cadre rivalry is sown. More specifically, which cadre members occupy how many positions, in which ministries/divisions and at what level come to the focus and the idyllic picture of distribution of posts among different cadres on some rational grounds disappears. Hence strong arguments are presented not only to restructure the cadre system but also the management system of the civil service as a whole. These arguments have also been linked with democratic governance system and accountability mechanisms within the civil service.

The Bangladesh Civil Service (BCS) Coordination Committee and Doctors, Engineers and Agriculturists (DEA) Combine, a conglomerate of all technical and professional cadres within the BCS and three professions presented proposals which if accepted would bring about fundamental changes in the way the cadre services are organized, affect promotional prospects of generalist cadre members and lead to partial reorganization of the civil service.

The demands of the BCS Coordination Committee and DEA Combine include the following (Hena, 1993):

a) creation of a professional Civil Service Ministry (CSM) in place of Ministry of Establishment (MOE);
b) according highest importance to specialization based on functions in relevant ministries;
c) all BCS cadres to meet functional requirements of the concerned ministry;
d) BCS (Administration) cadre be brought under relevant functional ministries by dividing this cadre into BCS (Land) and BCS (Magistracy) cadres to link BCS (Administration) cadre with its actual functions;

e) 95% of the posts of secretaries including posts in the Prime Minister's Secretariat, Cabinet Division and MOE be filled proportionally from among civil servants of all BCS cadres excepting BCS (Administration) ensuring representation of all professional groups within the civil service;
f) posts in the Planning Commission and the Bangladesh Public Service Commission (BPSC) have to be filled rationally from among concerned cadres and professions;
g) for encadrement of those professionals, i.e. engineers, doctors and agriculturists who are working in ministries without belonging to any cadre, clear function-based appointment policies have to be formulated and if needed new cadres be created;
h) ensuring formal participation of all cadres in policy formulation;
i) ensuring priority of officers having technical knowledge and expertise in every functional ministry and filling all posts from assistant secretary to secretary including field level posts of that ministry from among members of the concerned functional cadre;
j) removal of anomalies in the pay scales of different cadres as per recommendation of the cabinet sub-committee by restoring equity in pay as suggested by the 1977-78 National Pay Scale;
k) formulation of Senior Professional Administrative Scheme in line with U.K. model for senior members of all functional groups for appointment in high-level administrative and policy -planning posts;
l) establishment of a Combined Civil Service College (CCSC) for training of members of all professional groups within the civil service;
m) immediately measures should be taken to create equal opportunities for promotion of members of all cadres at all levels as most cadre members and professionals suffering from frustration due to lack of scope for promotion;
n) each pay in the national pay scale should be declared as a grade to implement the declared and accepted main policy of the government within the present administrative system in light of the reorganized service structure and be used to judge the status of the concerned officer in the revised Warrant of Precedence irrespective of the fact as to where he is working; and
o) declare minister as the chief executive of a ministry by changing the Rules of Business to ensure accountability of administration to the parliament and thereby institutionalizing democracy.

The arguments that BCS (Administration) officials provide is to justify the maintenance of the status quo in the cadre system with minor modifications. Their arguments are:

a) professional civil servants asking for double advantage -they want to retain promotional prospects in their own line and at the same time encroaching upon the secretariat posts which should normally be occupied by members of generalist cadres, specifically the BCS (Administration);
b) for appointment at different levels of positions starting from assistant secretary to secretary aptitude, training and career prospects should be clearly scrutinized;
c) appointment of professional civil servants in different ministries of different cadres are adversely affecting the promotional prospects of the BCS (Administration) cadre;
d) generalist officers to have the authority and opportunity to take high-level decisions as only they can assess better political and other considerations involved in such decisions;
e) distribution of secretariat posts amongst too many cadres has resulted in a scramble for a 'share of the pie' among functional and professional cadres and groups;
f) specialists be given recognition in their posts outside the secretariat and corresponding status; and
g) changes in Rules of Business may be undertaken to suit the changing political reality.

STATUS OF CADRE CIVIL SERVANTS

A structured questionnaire survey was administered by the author to the recent post-graduate students of the University of Dhaka. The main objective of the survey was to discern their attitude and opinions towards cadre civil service. More specifically, the students were asked to indicate whether they respected the cadre civil servants and would make a career as cadre civil servants given the opportunity.

The students were chosen on a random basis. Their total number was fifty-eight. For making the sample representative, the students were chosen from five faculties and two institutes of the University of Dhaka. The breakdown of the students were as follows: Biological Science -- 15, Social Science -- 13, Science -- 10, Commerce – 5, Arts – 5 Institute of Business Administration – 5 and Institute of Education and Research – 5.

The results of the findings indicated the following:

a) overwhelmingly large number of respondents, i.e. 52 felt that cadre civil servants were respected by people-at-large;
b) a large number of respondents, i.e. 37 opined that cadre civil servants were neither conscientious nor dedicated to their work;
c) a large number of respondents, i.e. 38 said they were neither efficient nor effective in their jobs;
d) important differences surfaced among respondents on the question of cadre civil servants involvement in corruption – 35 respondents held the view that most of them were involved in corruption in one form or another while rest did not subscribe to such a notion;
e) the respondents disagreed marginally when it came to judge the comparative qualifications of cadre civil servants and their counterparts in the private sector – 32 respondents stated that the cadre civil servants were as qualified and efficient as officials in private business while 26 felt that the latter were more qualified;
f) 39 respondents felt that cadre civil servants have more opportunity for career advancement compared to members of other services within the public service;
g) an overwhelming majority of the respondents, i.e. 42 agreed that cadre civil servants were getting lower salary and fewer other benefits compared to their counterparts in the private sector;
h) again a very large number of respondents, i.e. 46 stated that cadre civil servants enjoyed greater tenure of service than their counterparts in the private sector;
i) in terms of the nature of work, once again an overwhelming majority of the respondents, i.e. 43 considered the job of a cadre civil servant interesting; and
j) with regard to making a career as a cadre civil servant the response had been mixed – only 36 respondents would opt for a career in cadre civil services while the rest seemed not interested.

TRAINING

The state of public sector training is highly unsatisfactory. This situation has been further aggravated by continuous and steady decline in the standard of higher education and failure of successive governments to link training with career planning of civil servants. Training as a key segment of civil service management continues to receive lip service and almost no long-term policy commitment to enhance its effectiveness and quality. No wonder training is not taken seriously by anybody – trainees, trainers and policy makers – resulting in a situation of utter frustration for all concerned.

The specific problems which have contributed to lack of effectiveness of training are summarized below.

First, the design, implementation and evaluation of training programmes are neither adequate nor relevant in the context of the changing needs of civil servants (Khan and Siddiquee, 1997). Second, the training institutions lack qualified trainers, inadequate financial and other support, enjoy little freedom of action and are heavily dependent on guest lecturers. Third, in many cases the training institutions are headed and dominated by civil servants with no specialized training or interest in training. This practice of using training institutions as 'dumping grounds' for accommodating incompetent, undesirable and corrupt civil servants denies such institutions of effective leadership at the top and blocking promotional prospects of professional trainers within. Fourth, even after twenty-five years of independence, the country lacks a national training policy. Efforts were made to formulate such a policy in early '80s under the aegis of the then newly-constituted National Training Council (NTC). But the NTC did not succeed in its major task due mostly to bureaucratic resistance and bureaucratic maneuvering to exclude professionals in NTC to meaningfully contribute in the process to formulate a national training policy (Khan, 1984). Fifth, training institutions in Bangladesh lack professionalism (Khan and Zafarullah, 1980; Aminuzzaman, 1993). There is a general consensus that almost all public sector training institutions suffer from lack of qualified and experienced professional trainers. This lacunae is reflected in the design of courses, methods of instruction used and system of feedback. Courses are usually not designed keeping in mind the needs and requirements of trainees. So the utility of such courses is minimal at best. Lecture is the most commonly used method to communicate information and ideas in a training situation. Other methods that enable participants to involve more actively in the learning process are only used occasionally. The trainees responses to courses attended are collected through distribution of short forms but whether such feedback are utilized in changing and modifying course contents and instructional methods subsequently is open to question. Sixth, more importantly, the emphasis of most training courses is on the understanding of administrative techniques rather than on the improvement of human relation skills and broadening outlook of civil servants (Zafarullah and Khan, 1988).

Problems in public sector training can be attributed, to a large extent, in the way the training institutions are organized and managed. Training institutions have been set up to cater to the needs of a particular cadre or segments within the civil service system without giving adequate attention to their institutional and personnel requirements. As has been indicated earlier most training institutions have failed to attract and retain qualified and dedicated trainers and not been able to secure related material and other technical support. Multiplicity of training institutions with narrow mission and peripheral outlook have also resulted in duplicity of efforts and lack of coordination. These have put a tremendous pressure on the resources earmarked for the training area as well as for the personnel involved.

Training institutions are mostly controlled and directed by ministries. The Bangladesh Public Administration Training Centre (BPATC), the premier training institution in the country, which is responsible for conducting both post-entry and in-service training programmers for entry, mid-level and senior-level public servants is an attached department of the Ministry of Establishment (MOE). The BPAT.C was created in 1984 by merging the three erstwhile civil service training institutions, i.e. Civil Officers Training Academy (COTA), National Institute of Public Administration (NIPA) and Bangladesh Administrative Staff College (BASC) with the objectives of raising the quality and standard of training. But this has not happened because MOE controls, monitors and directs the activities of the BPATC leaving little room for the latter to undertake any activity on its own (Khan, 1986). The BPATC does not have much say in the selection of trainees. Many key positions, both directional and instructional in the training institutes are occupied by civil servants whose primary allegiance is to their cadres and controlling ministries rather than to the training institution they are supposed to serve. Selection of trainees is primarily the responsibility of concerned ministries. The dependence of the BPATC on the MOE ranges from administrative to financial matters. Other training institutions operating in the public sector are controlled in similar manner by their respective ministries.

TRANSFER

It is clear from the interviews conducted by the author that the government has no policy on transfer of cadre civil servants. The situation in the area of transfer shows a trend of uncertainty and lack of trust among civil servants and ministers. The frequency of transfer of civil servants at all levels is indeed astounding as the statistics pertaining to the cadre civil servants is shown below.

Only ten percent of the deputy secretaries, joint secretaries and additional secretaries completed two years in one post.

A staggering eighty percent of deputy secretaries, joint secretaries, additional secretaries stayed in one post for one year or less. Ten percent of deputy secretaries, joint secretaries, and additional secretaries who remain officer-on-special duty (OSD) are subjected to still more frequent transfer.

Fifty percent of the secretaries have been transferred within one year or within less than two years after assuming charge of a ministry or a division.

During the five year rule (1991-1996) of Khaleda Zia's BNP government changes at the level of secretaries was made 86 times breaking all past record in this regard (*Dhaka Courier*, 13 September 1996). The changes were brought about because many secretaries resisted political interference and opposed giving undue favour to BNP supporters.

A cadre civil servant's aptitude, training and relevant experience is not always taken into consideration while deciding on his/her transfer.

PROMOTION

It had been claimed to be a priority area by Khaleda Zia government. In support of its claim the government could very well point to mass promotion of 657 officers of different ranks in 1992. The massive exercise was purportedly taken to: (a) offset stagnation caused by non-promotion to the ranks of deputy and joint secretaries since 1985; and (b) to build a dynamic administration by reducing frustration among promotees. Recently, the new Awami League government of Sheikh Hasina also promoted a number of mid-ranking and senior civil servants.

Promotion in the cadre civil service is based on merit but seniority is given "due consideration". Promotion to deputy secretaries, joint secretaries, additional secretaries is based on the following formula. Sixty percent weightage is given on any ten years of a candidate's Annual Confidential Report (ACR) and forty percent weightage is placed on the interview. In interview both seniority and performance are considered. Serious doubts have been raised as to the validity of ACR and interview as mechanisms to meaningfully judge a candidate's potential and suitability for promotion.

Promotion is an area of civil service management where clash of interests among members of generalist cadres, specially BCS (Administration) and professional and functional cadres is the greatest. This is primarily because government has not as yet come up with a promotion policy covering all BCS cadres. For some eight cadres including health, general education, technical education, judicial and statistics promotion appears to be automatic and based on seniority only. On the other hand, revival of Promotion Examination Rule, 1986 has adversely affected the promotion prospects of a number of candidates belonging to some other cadres.

The massive promotion exercise undertaken in 1992 and later on by the Khaleda Zia government satisfied nobody. The members of functional cadres and professionals groups made their displeasure known publicly alleging partiality towards BCS (Administration) and demanding cancellation of the promotion order. Some cadre civil servants took legal recourse to challenge the entire promotion exercise. On the other hand, many members of the BCS (Administration) were utterly frustrated as they did not get promotion. According to some of them they were no worse than those of their cadre-mates who were promoted.

Table 4.5. Class-wise number of female officers and staff.

Class	Ministries/ Divisions (Secretariat)	Departments/ Directorates Corporations	Autonomous Bodies/	Total
(1)	(2)	(3)	(4)	(5)
Clas I	164	2,925	1,977	5,066
Class II	6	1,072	1,408	2,486
Class III	345	50,605	7,110	58,060
Class IV	199	8,746	3,480	12,425
Grand total	714	63,348	13,975	78,037

SOURCE: Ministry of Establishment, Statistics ofCivil Officers and Staff of GPRB, Dhaka, 1992.

Also there was no relation between promotion and posting. No advance thinking and planning was done in this regard. Many promotee officers had to wait as officer-on-special duty (OSD) for months before being posted. In a number of cases posts had to be upgraded to accommodate promotees. The nature and content of the jobs did not matter. Many corporations and autonomous bodies refused to accept promoted cadre civil servants within their realm causing undue delay in the former's placement.

WOMEN IN THE CIVIL SERVICE

The Indian Civil Service (ICS) was manned exclusively by men. The situation did not change significantly during united Pakistan

Table 4.6. Class-wise number of male and female civil servants.

CLASS	MIN/DIV		DEPT/DTE		AUTO/CORP		TOTAL	
	M (%)	F (%)	M (%)	F (%)	M (%)	F (%)	M (%)	F (%)
Class I	1,711	164	29,997	2,925	41,911	1,977	73,619	5,066
	(91.25)	(08.75)	(91.16)	(08.84)	(95.50)	(04.50)	(93.56)	(06.44)
Class II	45	6	9,669	1,072	24,658	1,408	34,327	2,486
	(88.23)	(11.77)	(90.02)	(09.98)	(94.60)	(05.40)	(93.26)	(06.74)
ClassIII	3,787	345	3,92,254	50,605	1,25,741	7,110	5,21,782	58,060
	(91.65)	(08.35)	(80.57)	(11.43)	(94.65)	(05.35)	(89.99)	(10.01)
Class IV	2,144	199	1,54,073	8,746	82,722	3,480	2,38,939	12,425
	(91.51)	(08.49)	(94.63)	(05.37)	(95.96)	(04.04)	(95.06)	(04.94)

SOURCE: Same as Table 4.1.

(1947-1971). Women were debarred from entering the Civil Service of Pakistan (CSP), the successor of the ICS, the Pakistan Foreign Service (PFS) and many other central and provincial class 1 civil services. Only a handful women entered a few class 1 services like the Pakistan Audit and Accounts Service (PAAS) and Pakistan Taxation Service (PTS). The main intention was to keep women confined to mostly desk-bound jobs. It was felt that women would not be suitable for such jobs that called for extensive field visits and inspection, maintenance of law and order and collection of revenues (Chowdhury, 1969: 105).

The position of women vis-a-vis men in terms of number is still insignificant (Tables 4.5 and 4.6). An analysis of the tables indicate that number of women holding class I positions in the ministries/divisions, departments/directorates and autonomous bodies/corporations is only 5,066 compared to 73,619 men. This means that 6.44% women are occupying class I positions compared to 93.56% men. The position of women performing mostly functions of clerical nature in class II is slightly better. But the situation of female employees in class IV doing cleaning and messengerial jobs is the worst in terms of their meagre number. The situation of women in 29 cadre services is by no means satisfactory (Table 4.7). Excepting for two cadres, i.e. Bangladesh Civil Serves (BCS) General Education and Health representation of women in other cadres is rather poor. In nineteen cadres number of women is less than 10 and in two cadres they have no representation at all. Data collected in 1989 (Table. 4.8) also show that number of women compared to men in seventeen important ministries and the President's Secretariat is far fewer. In terms of women's representation in 1988 at the higher levels of the civil service, i.e. secretary, additional secretary, joint secretary and deputy secretary, is almost non-existent (Table 4.9). The situation is little better at the entrance level of cadre officers, i.e. assistant secretary (Table 4.10). It is clear that even in 1993 women were not represented at he higher rungs of the civil service (Table 4.10). The position of women at the entrance level and at the next level, i.e. senior assistant secretary has somewhat improved in terms of their numerical number (Table 4.10).

Table 4.7 List of 29 cadres and the number of women officials in them (1972-1986).

Name of cadre	Number
Administration	112
Agriculture	7
Ansar	3
Audit & Accounts	7
Commerce	1
Cooperative	7
Custom & Excise	4
Economic	53
Family Planning	14
Fisheries	9
Food	3
Foreign Affairs	6
Forestry	4
Genral Education	680
Health	400
Information	22
Judiciary	42
Police	2
Livestock	8
Postal	4
Public Health Engineering	1
Public Works	1
Railway Engineering	0
Railway Communication & Commerce	2
Roads and Highways	0
Statistics	10
Telecommunication	1
Taxation	8
Technical Education	6
Total	1418

SOURCE: A.K.M. Huq and H. Bela, Women in Bangladesh Civil Service (in Bangla), Dhaka: Bangladesh Public Administration Training Centre, 1988.

Table 4.8. Position of women class I officers in seventeen imprtant ministries/president's secretariat in 1989

Name of the Ministry	Women Class I Officer	Male Calss I Officer
Agriculture	5	45
Commerce	4	43
Education	8	58
Establishment	5	91
Finance	5	198
Fisheries & Livestock	1	30
Food	1	35
Foreign	4	80
Health and Population Control	4	47
Home	1	40
Industry	2	53
Information	4	29
Labour & Manpower	3	23
Local Government & Rural Development	3	35
Planning	28	202
Presidents' Secretariat	7	135
Social Welfare	1	10
Women's Affairs	3	10

SOURCE: S. Khan, "Women in Bureaucracy: Bangladesh Perspective" in J. Huq et al. (eds.). *Women in Politics and Bureaucracy*. Dhaka: Women for Women, 1995.

Table 4.9. Representation of women at different levels in the civil service.

Position	Male	Female
Secretary and Additional Secretary	55	–
Joint Secretary	88	1
Deputy Secretary	168	1
Assistant Secretary	594	23

SOURCE: Ministry of Establishment, 1988.

Table 4.10. Rank/level distribution of women officers in the Bangladesh civil service administration cadre.

Rank/level	Number	Percentage
Secretary	–	–
Additional Secretary	–	–
Joint Secretary	–	–
Deputy Secretary	3	1.1
Senior Assistant Secretary	43	15.6
Assistant Secretary	230	83.3
Total	276	100

Discussions above indicate that no significant breakthrough has occurred in terms of female representation at the higher and lower levels of the civil service. Only at the entrance level some marginal improvements have taken place. For an understanding of this present situation pertaining to women in public service an attempt is made below to discuss some relevant variables.

Many variables (Khan, 1995: 139-144) influence the nature and extent of participation of women in the civil service. It is not intended to provide here a catalogue of all such variables rather the focus is on selected major variables which significantly affect women representation in the public service.

REPRESENTATION

The question of representation is very critical. Many countries of the world, whether developed or developing, are grappling with the thorny problem of how to increase representation of those segments of the society whose participation has been minimal in the civil service vis-a-vis their total number and the need to simultaneously uphold the criterion of merit in choosing and promoting public servants. So equity becomes a key concern in this context. But reconciling merit and equity is not always easy specially when there is increasing demand for efficient service from a civil service which is not merit-based and deficient in terms of structure and ethos.

At independence in December 1991 Bangladesh found that in its public service not only women but ethnic, religious groups and some of the regions were under represented. The constitution, as a result, indicated its faith in the broad tenets of equal employment opportunity, which were to govern the recruitment and selection of public personnel (Zafarullah and Khan, 1989:82). In fact, recognizing the urgency of the problem the government adopted quotas (reservation of posts) three months prior to the enactment of the constitution in December 1972.

This adoption was reflected in an interim recruitment policy. This was designed to achieve greater equity in the representation of all regions and groups in civil service by reservation of positions and giving preference to certain sections of the population (Zafarullah and Khan, 1989: 83). Specific quotas were prescribed for women 10% and affected women 5%, freedom fighters 30% and regions 35% leaving 20% for selection based on merit (Zafarullah and Khan, 1989:83). This policy had a number of dimensions. First, it recognized the need for greater participation of different disadvantaged groups, i.e. women and under-represented regions in the civil service. Second, it acknowledged the contribution of those who fought for the liberation of the country and those women who were adversely affected by the Pakistan army. But over the years changes have occurred in the quota due to policy changes of governments. At present in the quota system 10% of the posts are reserved for women in class I services. The Bangladesh Public Service Commission (BPSC) in its annual reports since 1990 has been urging the government to review the reservation policy pertaining to civil service jobs. The BPSC recommended that in view of extreme shortage of candidates belonging to freedom fighter category 30% posts reserved for them should be reallocated in the following manner:

i) reduction of freedom fighter quota from 30% to 5% for all gazetted and non-gazeted posts;
ii) redistribution of 25% of freedom fighter quota for gazetted posts by assigning 15% to merit and 10% reserving for women; and

iii) for non-gazetted posts the freedom fighter quota of 25% be redistributed giving 10% to women and 15% to be assigned on the basis of population.(Annual Report of PSC, 1995)

The Commission argued that a change in the government policy will encourage huge number of women in the country to be involved in productive and gainful employment (Annual Report of PSC, 1995). The Commission's optimism is well-ground in facts. The 1993 annual report of PSC indicated a healthy trend. Between the years of 1985 and 1992 women candidates not only competed in large numbers compared to the past but obtained selection for majority of posts reserved for them (Annual Report of PSC, 1993). The government is yet to take any policy decision about enhancement of quota for women in the civil service. In fact, government policy in this regard is characterized by indecision, confusion, delay and play-safe attitude.

TRAINING

Training is a vital component of civil service management. Renewal of knowledge base, updating of information and changes in attitudes of personnel are usually the broad goals of any training programme. This is one of the areas which has been almost totally neglected in the case of women civil servants of Bangladesh. Even today no training programme exists which would sensitize male civil servants about how to behave and work with their female colleagues. No policy decision has been taken by the government so far to include women-related components in the regular training programmes of class I civil servants belonging to the entry, mid-and higher levels. This has created difficulties for women to perform more meaningfully in their jobs.

An expert panel report recommended that to alleviate the present situation the following needs to be done.

> The establishment of a government policy to discourage harassment of women (sexual and other forms) and a process to permit redress for gricvances in this area; mandatory training programmes which

would focus on such subjects as gender in management, awareness development (for both men and women), and harassment (Report of Public Administration Sector Study in Bangladesh, 1993:92).

In other words, training programmers should be prepared in such a manner so that on completion of training male civil servants develop attitudes and working habits which are congenial for developing as well as maintaining relationships between male and female civil servants premised on mutual respect and understanding.

EDUCATION

Education is probably the most important variable which determines the extent of progress that a country can make in various fields. As has been indicated earlier the number of educated people are few in Bangladesh and the number of highly-educated ones are fewer still. The situation of women in the area of education is unsatisfactory to say the least.

Unless a significant breakthrough can be made in the area of female education and specially at the higher level no effort to increase the representation of women in the civil service will succeed. The Khaleda Zia government took a number of policy decisions to encourage female enrolment in both primary schools and high schools. But it is too early to make an assessment of such policy decisions and their impact on the number of female civil servants in the future. What needs to be done is not more policy statements but effective and timely implementation of policies that would substantially reduce the huge gender gap that exists in all levels in the area of education. Because only through such actions changes can be hoped to be brought about in the broad social milieu and may eventually lead to effective empowerment of women in all spheres of society including the civil service.

ASSESSMENT OF SIZE AND RELEVANCE OF THE CIVIL SERVICE

As has been shown in an earlier section that the size of the civil service in Bangladesh is small compared to many developing countries in Africa, Asia and Latin America. But it has also been pointed out earlier that the cost of maintaining such a civil service is rather high. Also there is increasing dissatisfaction as to the nature and quality of public services. It has also been seen that ministries and divisions have been created and maintained on political considerations rather than on sound management and financial considerations. Same is true about recruitment and retention of class III and class IV employees. It has been indicated in the Report of Martial Law Committee I (MLC-I) of 1982 and Report of the Administrative Reorganization Committee (ARC) of 1996 that Bangladesh does not require so many ministries/divisions and significant cut in their numbers as well as those working at class III and call IV levels is possible. Consequently, both the bodies recommended reduction of the number of ministries/divisions and lower-level secretariat-based employees. Even after the acceptance and implementation of MLC-I recommendations, the Ershad government backtracked because of political considerations and as a result number of ministries/divisions went up and freeze on public employment was lifted. The recently-submitted report of ARC is yet to be considered by the government.

Distribution of civil servants in various activities indicate among other things ratio of civil servants in terms of work to be performed and priorities of the government in regard to policies and programmes. But because of poor maintaince of records it is not possible to furnish clear breakdown in terms of deployment of cadre civil servants in various activities like district administration, law and order, local government, planning and development. But on the basis of interviews conducted by the author in 1994 it can be said that civil servants belonging to almost all 29 cadres are working at the district level. At the divisional level most of the 29 cadres are represented. Members of 15 to 16 cadres are working at thana level. It can also be added that in the area of law and order responsibility at the district level is shared by the deputy commissioner in the capacity of district magistrate who is a member of the BCS (Administration) cadre and superintendent of police who belongs to the BCS (Police) cadre. Planning activities both at the central level, i.e. in planning cells of various ministries and at the district level are undertaken by members of the BCS (Economic) cadre.

CONCLUSION

The discussion above makes it obvious that the present structure of Bangladesh civil service is not suitable for the task at hand and challenges that lie ahead. Also it has been shown that though the size of the civil service is small compared to a number of developing countries still personnel deployment among different classes and cadres have not been done on any scientific basis.

The management of the civil service in Bangladesh is highly centralized in terms of establishment control and planning practice. But advantages of continuing with such control and practice is highly doubtful. Lack of policies, narrow vision, opportunism and partisan attitude on the part of political and bureaucratic elites have created massive problems in the management of the civil service. All key areas within the civil service have been afflicted with multifarious problems. No significant effort has been made as yet to meaningfully solve such critical problems.

Increasing representation of women in the civil service in Bangladesh has not reached the desired stage. For that to happen basic changes need to be ushered in many areas including education. Successive governments have done very little to bridge the gap that exists among male and female civil servants in terms of numbers and opportunities. Lip service and tokenism still dominate the thinking of political elite in Bangladesh when it comes to increasing female representation in the civil service.

REFERENCES

Ahmed, S.G. (1985). "Framework of Personnel Administration in Bangladesh", *IJPA* 31(1): 50-56.

Ahmed, S.G. (1990). *Bangladesh Public Service Commission.* Dhaka: University of Dhaka.

Ahmed, S.G. and M.M. Khan (1990). "Bangladesh" in Subramaniam, V. ed. *Public Administration in the Third World.* New York: Greenword Press, pp.17-41.

Aminuzzaman, S.M. (1993). "Administrative Reforms and Their Impact on Training the Public Bureaucracy in Bangladesh", *Asian Review of Public Administration* 5(1): 24-42.

BPSC (1993). *Annual Report of the Bangladesh Public Service Commission.* Dhaka: Government of the People's Republic of Bangladesh (GPRB).

BPSC (1995). *Annual Report of the Bangladesh Public Service Commission.* Dhaka: GPRB.

Chowdhury, M.A. (1969). *The Civil Service of Pakistan.* Dhaka: National Institute of Public Administration.

Hena, M.A. (1993). "An Outline of Democratic Accountable Administration for Bangladesh". Dhaka: Doctors, Engineers and Agriculturists Coordination Committee.

Huq, A.K.M. and H. Bala (1988). *Women in Bangladesh Civil Service* (in Bangla). Dhaka: Bangladesh Public Administration Training Centre.

Khan, M.M. (1984). "The Need for a Comprehensive Training Policy in Bangladesh", *Management Development* 13(2): 54-59.

Khan, M.M. (1986). "Public Administration Training Centre : A Critical Overview" in M. M. Khan, and Husain, S.A. eds. Bangladesh: *Politics, Administration, Rural Development and Foreign Policy*. Dhaka: Centre for Administrative Studies, pp. 58-76.

Khan, M.M. (1994). "Bangladesh Public Service Commission: A Critical Overwiew", *Administrative Change* 22(1): 23-35.

Khan, M.M. (1995). "Women in Public Administration and Management: Bangladesh Experience", *The Chinese Public Administration Review* 4(3):127-150.

Khan, M.M. and H.M. Zafarullah (1980). "Public Administration Training in Bangladesh: An Overview", *IRAS* 56(4): 369-376.

Khan, M.M. and N.A. Siddiquee (1997). "Public Administration Education and Training in Bangladesh" in M.R. Davies et al. eds.

Public Administration Education: A Global Perspective. New York: Macmillan/Greenwood.

Khan, S. (1995). "Women and Bureaucracy: Bangladesh Perspective" in J. Huq et al. eds. *Women in Politics and Bureaucracy.* Dhaka: Women for Women, pp.71-85.

UNDP (1993). *Report on Public Administration Sector Study in Bangladesh.* New York: United Nations Development Programme.

World Bank, The (1996a). *Government that Works: Reforming the Public Service.* Washington, D.C.: The World Bank.

Zafarullah, H.M. and M.M. Khan (1988). "The Recruitment and Training of Administrative Elites in Bangladesh" in R.N. Thakur ed. *Elites: Paradigm and Change in Transitional Perspective.* New Delhi: Indian Institute of Public Administration, pp. 170-190.

Zafarullah, H.M. and M. M. Khan (1989). "Towards Equity in Public Employment", in Tummala, K.K. ed. *Equity in Public Employment Across Nations.* Lanham, MD: University Press of America, pp.79-102.

CHAPTER 5

Major Administrative Reform Initiatives in Bangladesh

INTRODUCTION

Major characteristics of civil service systems in British India and in Pakistan are very much present in the civil service system of Bangladesh. The bureaucratic culture is distinctly British and not suited to the needs of today's citizens in an independent country (chapter 3). The components of the bureaucratic culture continue to affect the functioning of the civil service and moulding the behavioural patterns of civil servants.

Bangladesh's inherited civil service system has undergone only cosmetic changes since independence of the country in 1971 despite formation of a number of high-powered commissions and committees by different governments to reform the public bureaucracy (Table 5.1). The bureaucracy is still characterized by centralization of authority at the top of the hierarchy , closed career concept, security of term, preponderance of the cadre system, elitist orientation, abundance of rules and regulations, lack of respect for common people and lack of service orientation.

The focus of the present chapter is to discuss and analyse the nature, composition and recommendations of major reform bodies as well as to review the implementation or non-implementation of recommendations of such reform bodies by successive governments. In terms of scope and focus, the committees and commissions can be placed into three more or less distinct categories -- broad, mid-range and narrow (Table 5.2). Reform bodies can also be categorized in terms of nature of their membership (Table 5.3). The discussions that follow indicate that among other things membership of the committees and the commissions were monopolized by civil servants either serving or retired -- here was almost no interest on the part of governments to make the memberships of reform bodies representative of the various segments of the society.

Table 5.1. Ccommittees and commissions appointed by governments to study different aspects of civil service and to recommend reform measures, 1971-1996

1. Civil Administration Restoration Committee (CARC)
   Appointed on 27 December 1971. Submitted its report on 4 January 1972
2. Administrative and Services Reorganization Committee (ASRC)
   Appointed on 15 March 1972. Submitted its reports in two phases in April 1973 and in May 1974
3. National Pay Commission I (NPC-I)
   Appointed on 20 February 1976. Submitted its main report on 27 May 1977
5. Martial Law Committee for Examining Organizational Set Up of Ministries/Divisions, Departments, Directorates and Other Organizations Under Them I (MLC-I)
   Appointed on 18 April 1982. Submitted its reports in phases between 31 May and August 1982.
6. Committee for Administrative Reorganization/Reform (CARR)
   Appointed on 28 April 1982. Submitted its report on 22 June 1982
7. Martial Law Committee for Examining Organizational Set Up of Public Statutory Corporations (Autonomous/Semi-Autonomous Bodies and Allied Organizations) II (MLC II)
   Appointed on 8 May 1983. Submitted its report on 29 February 1984
8. Committee for Examination of Irregularities in Appointment and Promotion of Officers and Staff in the Government (CEI)
   Appointed on 9 September 1982. Submitted its report on 17 April 1983
9. National Pay Commission II (NPC-II)

Table 5.1. Contd.

Appointed on 31 May 1984. Submitted its report in 1985

10. Secretaries Committee on Administrative Development (SCAD)
Appointed on 20 April 1985. Submitted its report in 1986
11. Special Committee to Review the Structure of the Senior Services Pool (SC)
Appointed on 23 December 1985. Submitted its report in 1986
12. Cabinet Sub-Committee (CSC)
Appointed on 3 June 1987. Submitted its report on 22 June 1989
13. National Pay Commission III (NPC-III)
Appointed in August 1989. Report submitted in 1990
14. Administrative Reorganization Committee (ARC)
Appointed in August 1993. Report of the Committee submitted in August 1996
15. National Pay Commission IV (NPC-IV)
Appointed in August 1996. Yet to submit it's report
16. Administrative Reforms Commission (ARC)
Appointed in December 1996.

SOURCE

M. M. Khan, *Politics of Administrative Reform: A Case Study of Bangladesh*. New Delhi: Ashish Publishing House, 1991.

M. M. Khan, *Civil Service Management in Bangladesh*. Dhaka : United Nations Development Programme, 1993.

M. M. Khan, *Civil Service Reform in Bangladesh : An Agenda for Change*. Dhaka: The World Bank, 1994.

M. M. Khan, 'Resistance to Administrative Modernization in Bangladesh' in A. Claisse and Marie-Christine Meininger eds. *Administrative Modernization*. Brussels: International Institute of Administrative Sciences, 1997.

Table 5.2. Scope and focus of committees and commissions appointed by Governments for reforming the Civil Service, 1971-1996

Scope	Focus	Committee/Commission
BROAD	Pay in the Civil Service Micro-restructuring within	National Pay Commission-I (NPC-I)

Scope	Focus	Committee/Commission
	the Civil Service	Martial Law Committee for examining organizational set-up of Ministries/Divisions, Departments, Directorates and other organizations under them-I (MLC-I)
	Entire Civil Service Local Governance	Administrative and Services Reorganization Committee (ASRC)
	Entire Civil Service pay in the Civil Service	Pay and Services Commission (P&SC)
	Local Governance	Committee for Administrative Reorganization/Reform (CARR)
	Entire Civil Service Local Governance	Administrative Reforms Commission (ARC)
MID-RANGE	Micro-Restructuring within the Civil Service	Martial Law Committee for Examining Organizational Set-Up of Public Statutory Corporations (Autonomous, Semi-Autonomous Bodies and Allied Organizations)-II (MLC-II)
	Pay in the Civil Service	National Pay Commission-II (NPC-II)
	Pay in the Civil Service	National Pay Commission-III (NPC-III)
	Pay in the Civil Service	National Pay Commission-IV (NPC-IV)
	Micro-Restructuring within the Civil Service	Administrative Reorganization Committee (ARC)
	Restoration of Civil Administration at Different Levels	Civil Administration Restoration Committee (CARC)
NARROW	Recruitment and Promotion in the Civil Service	Committee for Examination of Irregularities in Appointment and Promotion of Officers and Staff in the Government (CEI)
	Promotion of Cadre Civil Servants	Secretaries Committee on Administrativge Development (SCAD)
	Senior Services Pool	Special Committee to Review

Scope	Focus	Committee/Commission
		the Structure of the Senior Services Pool (SC)
	Senior Services Pool and Promotion of Cadre Civil Servants	Cabinet Sub-Committree (CSC)

SOURCE: Same as Table 5.1.

Table 5.3. Nature of membership of Committees and Commissions appointed by Governments to reform the Civil Service, 1971-1996.

Membership	Committees/Commissions	Composition
REPRESEN-TATIVE	Administrative and Services Reorganization Committee (ASRC)	Led by an academic, members included a parliamentarian, a civil servant and an academic
	National Pay Commission-II (NPC-II)	Headed by a judge, members included individuals from civil service, academic and private sector
CIVIL SERVANTS-DOMINATED		
	National Pay Commission-I (NPC-I)	Chaired by a civil servant, all members excepting one belonged to the civil service
	Pay and Services Commission	Chairman and all embers excepting one belonged to the civil service
	Secretaries Committee on Administrative Development (SCAD)	Monopolized by civil servants
	Administrative Reorganization Committee (ARC)	Chairman and all members belonged to the civil service
	National Pay Commission-II (NPC-IV)	Chairman and two full-time members were retired civil servants
	Administrative Reforms	Headed by a senior retired

Membership	Committees/Commissions	Composition
	Commission (ARC)	civil servant and majority members included retired and serving civil servants
MILITARY OFFICIALS DOMINATED		
	Martial Law Committee for Examining Organizational Set Up of Ministries/ Divisions, Departments, Directorates Under Them (MLC-I)	Chairman and all other members excepting one were senior officers of the army
	Martial Law Committeefor Examining Organizational Set Up of Public Statutory Corporations (Autonomous/ Semi-Autonomous Bodies and Allied Organizations-II) (MLC-II)	Chairman and all members excepting two were senior army officers
CIVIL SERVICE-MILITARY		
	Special Committee for Administrative Reorganization-Reform (CARR)	Headed by the Chief of Navy and membership included four senior civil servants, a senior civil servant-turned minister, a senior army officer and an academic
	Committee for Examination of Irregularities in Appointment and Promotion of Officers and Staff in the Government (CEI)	Headed by a senior civil servant and other members included one senior army officer and three senior civil servants
	National Pay Commission -III (NPC-III)	Chaired by a senior civil servant and membership included three senior civil servants and one senior army officer

Membership	Committees/Commissions	Composition
POLITICIAN-DOMINATED		
	Cabinet Sub-Cimmittee (CSC)	All three members including chairman were senior ministers

SOURCE: Same as Table 5.1.

MUJIB ERA: GRANDIOSE VISION YET FUTILE EXERCISE

The Awami Leauge (AL) government headed by Sheikh Mujibur Rahman (Mujib) assumed power in liberated Bangladesh. The AL in October 1970 won a landslide victory in the first ever general elections in united Pakistan capturing 167 out of 169 seats in the National Assembly from the then East Pakistan. The massive victory of AL in the elections transformed it as the only political party to represent the interests of Bengalis. At independence the AL formed a government on the basis of its 1970 electoral victory and Mujib assumed the leadership of both the party and the government as the unquestioned leader of Bengalis in early 1972 on his return to Bangladesh from a prison in Pakistan.

The Mujib government appointed three reform bodies, i.e. two committees and one commission during its three and a half years rule between December 1971 to August 1975.

CIVIL ADMINISTRATION RESTORATION COMMITTEE (CARC)

Within two weeks of liberation of Bangladesh from occupation of Pakistani armed forces, a Committee was appointed to facilitate restoration of civil administration in a war-ravaged and strife-torn country. The body known as the Civil Administration Restoration Committee (CARC) was constituted on 27 December 1971. All six members of the Committee including the chairman were civil servants. Hence it was an in-house and bureaucrat-dominated Committee.

Mission

The CARC was given the responsibility to: (a) examine and suggest ways for restoration of field administration; (b) fix priorities and phases under which restoration of the administration may be implemented; (c) suggest ways for absorption of all employees and amalgamation of offices of Pakistan government with Bangladesh government; and (d) consider any other aspect of civil administration that the committee may consider desirable and necessary (Report of CARC, Part 1, 1972, p.9).

Significant Recommendations

The significant recommendations of the Committee included: (a) establishment of twenty ministries, three other secretariat organizations and seven constitutional bodies; (b) detail specification of functions of civil servants at sub-divisional, district and divisional levels; and (c) providing appropriate status and respect to officers and staff of civil administration as lawful organs of the government (Report of CARC, Part 1, 1972, pp. 2-8). The Committee felt that civil administration of the country should be premised on such guiding principles as democracy, socialism and secularism.

Outcome

Many recommendations of CARC were accepted by the government. This resulted in a reorganized secretariat with twenty ministries and a number of divisions, departments and other agencies under them. Implementation of other recommendations led to the formation of certain constitutional bodies like the Supreme Court, the High Court, the Public Service Commission, the Election Commission and the Office of Comptroller and Auditor General. The government did not accept CARC's recommendation to set up an Ombudsman. Most of the recommendations made by the Committee and accepted by the government were of interim nature and intended to put in place an administrative system at different levels in the model of the system that existed in the united Pakistan.

It needs to be pointed out that in view of the Committee's mandate, composition and time constraint much could not be expected from its deliberations.

ADMINISTRATIVE AND SERVICES REORGANIZATION COMMITTEE (ASRC)

On 15 March 1972 a four-member Administrative and Services Reorganization Committee (ASRC) was appointed. The chairman of the Committee was a noted political scientist, a distinguished public administration scholar and Vice Chancellor of the University of Dhaka. The other members were a US-trained economist and a member of the Planning Commission, a parliamentarian belonging to the ruling party and a senior generalist civil servant of the elite Civil Service of Pakistan (CSP) and Secretary, Cabinet Affairs. The last member was also assigned the additional responsibility to act as secretary to the Committee.

Mission

The ASRC was asked:

(a) to consider the present structure of various services . . . and determine the future structure keeping in view the fundamental needs and requirements of the government;

(b) to consider the amalgamation of all civil services … into one unified service;

(c) to determine the principles of integration of the personnel of various services in the new structure and to determine inter se seniority of personnel of the different services having similar academic background and job experiences in the process of merger or amalgamation, in some cases structural changes envisioned;

(d) to determine the future recruitment policy in the government services at various levels keeping in view the educational and other job requirements; and

(e) to prepare and recommend a comprehensive scheme for administrative reorganization (Report of ASRC, Part 1, 1973, pp. iii-iv)

Diagnosis

The ASRC was severely critical of the public service. It observed that "the existing services were divided into too many distinct entities with artificial walls built around them with varying career prospects, lacking in professionalism and too much class and rank-oriented with very little opportunities to rise to the top for those who started their career in the lower ranks" (Report of ASRC, Part 1, 1973, p. iv). The above observations made by ASRC almost a quarter century ago remains valid even today. The wide-ranging review of the state of affairs of the public service also found that the service structure was tailor-made to suit a colonial, capitalist and federal governmental system. Obviously, the situation was in clear contrast with the needs and aspirations of a country which was independent, socialist and unitary. The service structure was outdated, indolent and not responsive to the demands of the citizens. The procedures further added to the problems as these were complex, ponderous and confusing.

Significant Recommendations

The ASRCs recommendations had to be fundamental in nature as it attempted to lay the foundation of a modern civil service capable to cope with the multifarious problems facing a new, independent and war-ravaged country. The Committee made a number of significant recommendations which influenced and shaped the deliberations of committees and commissions appointed later on.

First, the Committee felt that division between former All-Pakistan and other Central Superior Services and the former Provincial Services as well as division between higher and lower classes be abolished and a continuous grading system from top to bottom should be substituted in each occupational group (Report of ASRC, Part 1, 1973, p. 26).

Second, the Committee suggested that reservation of posts for various groups within the public service should be discontinued.

Third, all public servants, the ASRC recommended, should be organized in a single classes unified grading structure (UGS) covering the whole public service. The UGS would comprise of ten grades with appropriate number of pay levels matching different levels of skill and responsibility premised on job analysis (Report of ASRC, Part 1, 1973, p. 26).

Fourth, to inculcate professionalism in the public service, the Committee suggested, division of all posts within it into two broad categories to be designated as Functional Posts and Area Group Posts (Report of ASRC, Part 1, 1973, pp. 34-35). The occupants of the first category posts would possess pre-entry technical and vocational education and also those who would have to acquire necessary technical and vocational qualifications after joining their positions. The second group would consist of such posts that would not require any single functional expertise but relevant experience and necessary training for holding them.

Fifth, the ASRC called for designating posts in top three grades, i. e. I, II and III as Senior Policy and Management Posts and tightening selection procedure for entrance into senior management positions (Report of ASRC, Part 1, 1973, pp. 37-38).

Sixth, the Committee also suggested a detail plan as to how its proposal for UGS be implemented throughout the public service. The plan included: (i) commissioning of a major study to work out details of UGS and prepare a time schedule for its implementation; (ii) creation of an Administrative Management and Reforms Division (AMRD) with a permanent secretary as head by reorganizing and expanding the then O&M Wing of the Establishment Division; (iii) placing the AMRD under the day-to-day supervision of a junior minister with the Prime Minister retaining the overall responsibility for it; and (iv) appointing a high-powered Implementation Committee under the chairmanship of a judge of the Appellate Division of the Supreme Court with two parliamentarians, chairmen of two Public Service Commissions and Secretaries of the Ministries of Finance, Law, Personnel Division and proposed Administrative Management and Reforms Division as members to provide guidelines to the work of AMRD (Report of ASRC, Part 1, 1973, pp. 46-47).

Seventh, the ASRC felt that individuals should be recruited to various grades in the public service on the basis of merit as tested by their performance in competitive public examinations. Persons with proven competence be appointed to technical posts laterally.

Eighth, in the area of training, the Committee made a number of recommendations that included: (i) creation of Training Wing in the Personnel Division to formulate a general training policy and promote and coordinate training programmes of ministries and departments; (ii) setting up of separate institutes for post-entry training of young recruits and senior administrators and strengthening the facilities of the institution responsible for mid-career training.

Ninth, in the area of central personnel management the ASRC made a lot of important recommendations. These included: (i) creation of a Personnel Division attached to the Office of the Prime Minister staffed by professionally competent persons to undertake a variety of responsibilities in the areas of staffing, job analysis and evaluation, training and career planning; (ii) establishing a personnel cell in each ministry and department; (iii) promotions to higher positions be given on the basis of merit as demonstrated in appropriate examinations and recommendations of relevant departmental promotion committees, and (iv) a civil servant be allowed to remain in a given job for at least two years (Report of ASRC, Part 1, 1973, pp. 96-107).

The ASRC also made a number of specific recommendations to democratize the governance system and reduce the powers and functions of the central government civil servants operating at field level positions (Khan, 1991, pp. 58-59).

First, increasing devolution of power and authority to elected local governments at different levels – district, thana and union was forcefully argued to enable locally-elected officials to provide leadership in developmental activities without interference from central government officials placed in the field. The local government was visualized to levy taxes within its jurisdiction and receive grants from the central government. A Local Government

Service to be created whose members would operate in local level only. The functions of key official of the central government in the district, i.e. the deputy commissioner, would be reduced.

Second, different local level field tiers had to be rationalized with upgradation of subdivisions into districts and abolition of divisions.

Third, separation of the judiciary from the executive had to be ensured for successful functioning of a democratic polity.

Fourth, at the central level the role of the secretariat needed to be restricted to: policy formulation, planning and evaluation of the executed plans and programmes.

Outcome

The ASRC submitted its recommendations to the government in two phases. But there was no official response to the Committee's work till the end of the Mujib government. It is difficult to understand why far-reaching recommendations of ASRC was shelved in spite of the fact that excepting the member-secretary all members including the chairman were close to Mujib both politically and personally. It is on record that Mujib was unhappy with the poor performance or lack of commitment of many senior civil servants. He knew the problems but did not want to go all the way to solve the malices. That created the paradox and consequently Mujib's lack of action.

But what is known is that senior generalist civil servants did not like the contents of the reports of the Committee. The leadership to resist the acceptance and the implementation of ASRC's recommendations was given by the senior members of the erstwhile CSP and spearheaded by the CSP Association. The implementation of ASRC's recommendations would have resulted (Khan, 1991: 82) in abolition of their privileged position in terms of promotion and posting and opened up greater opportunities to functional and specialist civil servants within the domain of the public service and also contributed to the effective political control of civil servants. The CSP Association submitted a representation to the Committee containing a set of its demands. These included: opposition to amalgamation of different civil services into one; sought reservation of all key posts in the secretariat and majority of field-level positions for its members as in the past; and wanted its nomenclature to be changed to Bangladesh Administrative Service (BAS) in line with Indian Administrative Service (IAS) (Khan and Zafarullah, 1982).

Also by the time the last report was submitted in mid-1974 Mujib's control over population at large and politics in particular became uncertain. Opponents to his government got organized. Economy started to slide due to the combination of factors including famine, mismanagement and inability to get required funds and aid from international donors and foreign countries. All these led Mujib to depend more heavily on senior civil servants to run the country. Some of the senior civil servants found this opportunity heaven-sent to consolidate and strengthen their positions vis-a-vis the government and ward off any attempt to restructure the civil service system.

National Pay Commission (NPC-I)

A National Pay Commission (NPC-I) was appointed on 21 July 1972 under the chairmanship of a retired secretary to the government. Besides the chairman, there were nine other members. The membership of the Commission included three full-time and five part-time members. The full-time members were all retired individuals with background in banking, police and technical education. The part-time members were all public servants, excepting one, representing such organizations as the Planning Commission, the Ministry of Finance, the Ministry of Defence, and the House Building Finance Corporation. A senior civil servant belonging to the erstwhile CSP was made member-secretary to the NPC-I.

Mission

The National Pay Commission (NPC-I) was assigned with a number of tasks. These included:

> (a) reviewing the pay structure of all employees in the public sector keeping in view the government's policy of socialism; and (b) recommending rationalization and standardization of pay scales of those who served under erstwhile central and provincial governments (Report of NPC-I, 1973, p. 1).

In addition, the Commission was asked to keep in mind a number of variables while making its recommendations. Those variables included: cost of living, resources at the disposal of the government, need to reduce disparity between the highest and the lowest income earners, need to attract and retain in the public sector highly talented technically and professionally qualified persons, the requirements of efficiency, equity and incentives for work and demand and supply relating to different professions and occupations (Report of NPC-I, 1973, p.1).

The Commission was also to work in close co-operation with the Administrative and Services Reorganization Committee (ASRC).

Diagnosis

It is clear from the above that NPC-I was given a difficult job. On the one hand, it had to come up with such recommendations, as would attract the best possible candidates but on the other the twin requirements of meager resources at the disposal of the government and the need to minimize the gap between the highest and the lowest income groups in the society to be kept in mind.

The NPC-I found a number of inadequacies and anomalies in the pay structure at that time. There were multiplicity of scales as well as diversity. The Commission identified as many as 2200 different scales of pay throughout the government. The situation was further complicated by diversity that existed in rates of increment and efficiency bars for similarly classified jobs (Khan, 1991, p. 54). It was noticed that though for majority of the posts time scales of pay were available, their time span varied significantly from two to twenty-five years.

Significant Recommendations

The guiding principles followed by NPC-I in recommending a rational pay structure were a livable wage, social acceptability, functionally distinguishable levels of responsibility matched with standardized pay levels and motivation based on patriotic grounds (Khan, 1991:59). The NPC-I felt that a nine-tier, administrative structure with corresponding pay scales could meet the requirements of a rational structure in Bangladesh during next five years, i.e. 1973-1978 (Obaidullah, 1995:141). Of the nine scales four would be normal direct entry tiers, three promotion tiers and two conversion tiers (Obaidullah, 1995:141). But the Commission's plan had to be modified to bring it in line with ASRC's recommendations. Eventually, the NPC-I recommended ten scales of pay to suit the ten service grades proposed by the ASRC.

Outcome

Some of the recommendations of the Commission were partially implemented. However, majority of the recommendations of the NPC-I were not implemented. Reasons can be offered as to why the Commission's recommendations suffered such a fate. First, compression of 2200 scales into 10 scales was very difficult task and it proved to be so at the implementation stage. Second, no major segment within the civil service supported the recommendations. Rather almost everybody who mattered opposed it. They felt that the NPC's recommendations were not based on proper evaluation of responsibilities of a particular scale and the corresponding pay. It has been stated that 'supervisory posts were downgraded in terms of pay and equalized with the grades of the supervised, creating deleterious effects on efficiency, morale and performance' (Obaidullah, 1995; 145). One of the consequences of such a situation was discontent and dissatisfaction among public servants. A large segment of public servants went to the court to challenge the implementation of NPC-I's recommendations and the verdict of the judiciary in most cases supported their standpoint (Report of Pay and Service Commission, 1977, p. 8).

ZIA ERA: CAUTIOUS MOVE TO MAINTAIN THE STATUS QUO

The first military ruler of Bangladesh was Lieutenant-General Ziaur Rahman (Zia). Zia, a freedom fighter and a shrewd tactician, captured power in September 1975. Zia's accession to power was aided by a number of factors including his popularity among soldiers and support provided by key faction leaders within the army. A number of coups and counter coups between August-September 1975 created a chaotic situation within the army and facilitated the process of Zia's assumption of state power. One of the key casualties of the coups was the founding father of the nation Sheikh Mujibur Rahman and most members of his immediate family. They were all killed. Zia's stay in power lasted little over five and a half years (September 1975 to May 1981). Zia continued with the presidential system introduced by Mujib. But he allowed political parties their normal activities reversing Mujib's decision to rule the country with one party, i.e. Bangladesh Krishak Sramik Party (BASAL). In the process Zia deliberately allowed anti-liberation and fundamentalist forces to gain a foothold in Bangladesh politics. This was a calculated move. Zia wanted to consolidate all forces opposed to the Awami League and thereby strengthen his position. His economic policy was premised on free flow of market forces. This was in contradiction to Mujib's socialist ideology. Zia also introduced an ideology 'Bangladeshi Nationalism' to counter Mujib's Bengali Nationalism.

PAY AND SERVICES COMMISSION (P&SC)

The Pay and Services Commission (P&SC) was set up on 20 February 1976. The Commission was composed of thirteen members including the chairman. The P&SC was headed by a retired Secretary to the government. There were full-time and part-time members as well as departmental representatives. Four were part-time members and all of them were retired senior civil servants with background in civil, finance, police and judicial services. Of the three part-time members one was a senior Secretary to the government, another was a retired chief engineer and the last one came from the private sector. There were four departmental representatives in the Commission as members. They represented the Ministries of Industries, Education and Establishment Division and Planning Commission. The original member- secretary was changed in mid-way and was replaced by another senior civil servant. It has been alleged that the first member-secretary attempted to alter the recommendations of the Commission in favour of members of the former CSP cadre. The mischief was detected in time and the chairman and members asked the government to withdraw him. The government complied with the request of the Commission. He was promptly replaced.

Mission

The Pay and Services Commission (P&SC) was asked to: (a) examine the existing pay and service structure of public sector employees excluding the defense services but including the civilians paid out of defence estimates and the employees of autonomous and semi-autonomous bodies, statutory corporations, the universities (excluding teaching posts) and nationalized enterprises excluding workers; (b) recommend a suitable service structure for the civil services along with their method of recruitment, training and deployment; (c) devise rational and simple principles for the amalgamation of employees of the erstwhile central and provincial governments performing similar duties and functions; and (d) recommend suitable pay structure including fringe benefits for civil services and employees of autonomous and semi-autonomous bodies, statutory corporations, universities (excepting teaching posts) and nationalized enterprises (Report of P&SC, Vol. 1, 1977, p. 7).

In making its recommendations pertaining to pay the Commission was instructed to take into consideration a number of factors including: (a) functional needs and requirements of the government; (b) job requirements for various services and posts; (c) cost of living; (d) resources of the government and public sector enterprises; (e) reduction of disparity between the highest and the lowest salary level; (f) attracting and retaining highly talented, trained, professionally and technically qualified persons in the public sector; (g) maintenance of efficiency, equity and incentives for work; and (h) demand and supply of various professions and occupations (Report of P&SC, Vol. 1, 1977, pp. 7-8).

The members of the P&SC were also asked to appraise themselves of the recommendations made earlier by ASRC and NPC-I and actions taken by the government to implement the recommendations of the latter. The Commission was directed to work in close cooperation with a commission appointed to recommend an appropriate pay structure for members of the armed forces.

The P&SC was given a rather broad mandate. It had the onerous task of examining both service and pay matters of all employees in the traditional public sector. This had to be accomplished within a given set of constraints. Added to these problems the expectations were high as to what the Commission would accomplish through its work. In other words, the Commission members had their hands full.

Diagnosis

Administrative inefficiency, the P&SC discerned, as one of the major factors damaging the prospect of planned development of the civil service. It, like the ASRC, termed the status of erstwhile constituted civil services as ambiguous primarily because the government at independence did not clarify the position of the CSP vis-a-vis other services. The practice of reservation of posts for those belonging to the CSP and denying entry of members of other services into its privileged domain enabled the CSP to monopolize key positions at the expense of other services which contributed to the creation and sustenance of a distinct and privileged class of elite civil servants. The Commission opined that development of the country depended on raising the status of the specialists and discontinuation of the CSP as a cadre.

Significant Recommendations

In making the recommendations, the Pay and Services Commission (P&SC) realized the complexities involved in running the modern government and the requirements of such a government. It understood that an all-purpose civil service had to be built with individuals possessing technical and scientific qualifications as well as those who were intellectually gifted and capable of working under political direction.

The P&SC made a number of significant recommendations covering wide areas within the broad canvass of the civil service.First, merit should be the sole determinant for appointment in the civil service and advancements therein and a system should be devised to ensure proper identification of the meritorious one (Report of P&SC, Vol.1, 1977, p. 287).

Second, the meaning of the term civil service was clarified. The term civil service should include all functioning in the traditional government sector, excluding those who are in the military (Report of P&SC, Vol. 1, 1977, p. 287).

Third, the barrier between the erstwhile CSP and other specialist and non-specialist services should be removed by effectuation of equal initial scales of pay and ensuring equitable opportunities for advancement to the top for all (Report of P&SC, Vol. 1, 1977, p.287).

Fourth, a Superior Policy Pool (SPP) to be designated as the open structure consisting of posts requiring all-round experience, administrative leadership and high-level coordination be constituted at the top of the civil service with brighter officers drawn from all branches of the civil service on the basis of merit and proven ability (Report of P&SC, Vol.1, 1977, p. 287).

Fifth, for the major functional areas of the government, cadre concept should be accepted and adopted. Organized cadre service should be formed at the top of the civil service.

Sixth, the civil service in Bangladesh should consist of four tiers with administrative, top management and specialist at the top and messengerial and custodian group at the bottom of the ladder with executive and middle management group and ministerial, inspectorial, technical and support group in between. The top most tier and the one following that tier be designated as levels A&B. A level cadre should be constituted with twenty-nine services.

Seventh, promotion policy to be formulated in such a way so as to encourage those with productivity and high caliber to reach the top.

Eighth, the Ministry of Establishment should be abolished. In its place, a Civil Service Ministry should be established and placed under the supervision of the head of the government with an O&M Division, a Training and Career Planning Division and a Recruitment and Service Management Division (Report of P&SC, 1977, Vol. 1, p. 290). The Civil Service Ministry should constantly review and advice the head of the government on the machinery of the government and the needs for adjustment (Report of P&SC, Vol. 1, 1977, p. 290). At the same time, the responsibility for recruitment and management of twenty-nine constituted services should be given to the particular administrative ministry while the Civil Service Ministry would manage the Superior Policy Pool (Report of P&SC, Vol.1, 1977, p.290). One of the major tasks of the Civil Service Ministry would be to undertake comparative research to keep itself familiar with experiences in civil service management in other countries.

Finally, 52 scales of pay were recommended to reduce the multiplicity of pay scales as well as to allow alternative scales for particular categories without disturbing the overall pay structure (Khan, 1991, p. 60). The Commission felt that two things needed serious consideration and action. Individuals with appropriate qualifications and background should be adequately remunerated. Upgradation and proper evaluation of those jobs that needed creativity and imagination had to be undertaken on a priority basis.

Outcome

The government moved slowly and contiguously to consider and implement some of the key recommendations of the P&SC. It took the government two years to implement in modified forms the Commission's accepted recommendations. The process was long. Five cabinet committees worked out the modalities of reform implementation.

First, twenty eight services under fourteen main cadres were created within the civil service. This action by the government signaled its acceptance in principle of the cadre concept.

Second, the government in 1977 provided for twenty-one scales of pay through the introduction of New National Grades and Scales of Pay (NNGSP). In the process the government drastically scaled down the number, i.e. fifty scales of pay which P&SC recommended. But the NNGSP satisfied very few people. Civil servants showed their displeasure utilizing various strategies. Strikes, meetings and demonstrations had adverse impact on the administration. Many civil servants felt injustice had been done to them in fixing pay scales. Protests came from all categories of employees. Professionals felt ignored as their rightful status was not reflected in the pay scale. They believed that this mischief was the handiwork of senior generalist civil servants.

Finally, a Senior Services Pool (SSP) was constituted by the government. The SSP was modeled in light of the P&SC's call for creation of a Superior Policy Pool (SPP). But the SSP Order was formulated and implemented in such a manner that the objective behind SSP was willfully ignored. Induction of a large number of mid-ranking and senior generalist civil servants without examinations and proper screening violated the very principles on which the SSP was premised. Initially only three civil servants belonging to specialist cadres were allowed to join the SSP. This action seriously undermined the credibility of the SSP in the eyes of non-generalist civil servants. This action, i.e. automatic induction of generalist civil servants into the SSP clearly demonstrated the enormous power of the generalist civil servants vis-a-vis others within the civil service system.

ERSHAD ERA: MANOEUVRING WITH LIMITED RESULT

Lieutenant-General Hossain Mohammad Ershad (Ershad) the then chief of Army Staff captured power in March 1982. Ershad's accession to power was a well-planned move. He took his time and judged the situation well. Justice Abdus Sattar, the hand-picked Vice President of General Zia succeeded him to the presidency through a presidential election. But Sattar proved to be inadequate to contain factions within the ruling Bangladesh Nationalist Party (BNP) and corruption among ministers. The BNP was in disarray in terms of leadership, factionalism, mismanagement and wide-ranging corruption. Ershad seized the situation to his advantage. He started talking openly to the press about militay's role in running the state. This move was intended to consolidate his position within the military as well as to put pressure on hapless Sattar to create institutional mechanisms to formally recognize and accommodate military's interests within the country's highest policy making body.

As soon as Ershad took over control of the country he made a number of promises which included the familiar ones like transferring power to civilians, ending corruption, streamlining administration and decentralization of power. There was very little new in Ershad's promises. Military dictators as a ritual make such promises when they capture power in developing countries.

In this section a number of reform initiatives undertaken during the Ershad era will be discussed. One of the important reform body's deliberations will not be considered here. The Committee for Administrative Reorganization/Reform (CARR) is the body in question. Its recommendations relate totally to the democratization of the governance system at the local and sub-national levels and its linkages with the national politico-administrative system. Here as our focus is on the reform efforts of the national civil service it will not be relevant to include CARR in the discussions that follow.

Beside CARR, a number of committees and two pay commissions were appointed. The committees included two martial law committees, a committee on irregularities, a secretaries committee a special committee, a cabinet sub-committee and a council committee.

Martial Law Committee-I

A five-member Martial Law Committee for Examining Organization Set Up of Ministries/Divisions, Departments, Directorates and Other Organizations Under Them (MLC) was appointed on April 18, 1982 under the chairmanship of a Brigadier. The other members of the Committee were two Lieutenant-Colonels, one Major and one mid-ranking civil servant. The latter was made secretary to the Committee.

Mission

The Committees's responsibilities included:

a. to review and recommend charter of duties of various Sections, Branches, Wings, Divisions and Departments;
b. to scrutinize existing and sanctioned manpower . . . to actual requirement;
c. to record observations on administrative inefficiency, irregularities and recommend steps to improve efficiency; and
d. to suggest rationalization of organization and functions of Ministries/Divisions, Departments and related organizations (Report of MLC-I, Phase 1, 1982, p. 45).

Diagnosis

The members of MLC observed that some senior civil servants made it a practice to approach the chief executive directly for creation of new ministries and divisions and expansion of the size of the new ones ignoring the Ministry of Establishment. This practice contributed to unnecessary increase in the number of civil servants. The Committee made a cryptic comment about the situation obtaining at that time 'the Parkinson's law about proliferation of organizations found its full play in Bangladesh' (Report of MLC-I, Phase 1, 1982, p. 9). The MLC found that attempts were made deliberately to bypass the Public Service Commission to recruit departmentally persons with lower qualifications and of lesser merit as compared to the requirements of the positions. Many instances of inefficiencies, irregularities and concentration of administrative and financial powers at the top echelons of the hierarchy were also noticed.

Significant Recommendations

The MLC made a number of recommendations pertaining to its area of investigation. These included among others:

a. reduction in the number of ministries/divisions, constitutional bodies/commissions, departments/directorates/subordinate offices, public statutory corporations and the personnel within;
b. delegation of administrative and financial powers down the hierarchy;
c. reduction of layers for deciding cases in the secretariat and fixing the supervisory ratio to 1:3;
d. formalizing and regularizing the recruitment process;
e. emphasizing on the merit principle for promotion of civil servants;
f. arranging training for civil servants;
g. finalizing seniority of cadre civil servants; and
h. setting up of a Public Accounts Committee (Report of MLC-I, Phase 1, 1982, pp. 35-42).

The government acted promptly on the recommendations of the MLC. A body was constituted in July 1982 titled Finalization of the Reorganization of Ministries/Divisions and Public Statutory Corporations (FRMDPSC) to review the recommendations of the MLC-I and to finalize the revised organizational set up of ministries/divisions/directorates and statutory corporations. The FRMDPSC was chaired by a Major General, its members included Secretary of the concerned ministry/division, Additional Secretary, O&M Wing, Establishment Division and a Brigadier. The FRMDPSC submitted its recommendations within the stipulated time, i.e. August 1982.

Outcome

The government almost immediately began the process of implementation of MLC-I's many recommendations after receipt of the FRMDPSC's observations and comments on the former. The implementation of MLC-I's recommendations resulted in the reduction of the number of ministries from 36 to 19, that of departments/directorates and subordinate offices form 243 to 181 and that of constitutional bodies and commissions from 12 to 9. The number of officials and employees working in different ministries/divisions mostly at the lower levels was reduced from 9,440 to 3,222. This was done by identifying surplus manpower and rationalizing duties and responsibilities of concerned officials and employees.

Martial Law Committee-II

A Martial Law Committee for Examining Organizational Set Up of Public Statutory Corporations (Autonomous/Semi-Autonomous Bodies and Allied Organizations) (MLC-II) was constituted on 8 May 1983. The MLC-II had originally six members but two other were subsequently coopted as members. The Committee was headed by a Brigadier the other members were four Lienteutant Colonels, one Major, one Joint Secretary and one Deputy Secretary. The latter was asked to act as the member-secretary to the MLC-II.

Mission

The MLC-II's responsibilities included:

a. to examine the organizational structure in relation to the aims and objectives of the organizations;
b. to review /revise the charter of duties of the functionaries of the organizations;
c. to examine the staffing pattern of the organizations;
d. to rationalize the organizational structure; and
e. to record observations on management problems , administrative inefficiency, irregularities and recommend remedial measures (Report of MLC-II, 1984, p. 2).

The MLC-II took into cognizance the report of another committee set up earlier under the chairmanship of the Cabinet Secretary. This committee looked into public statutory organizations also. It made certain observations and recommended abolition/merger/amalgamation in certain cases.

Diagnosis

The MLC-II observed that public statutory organizations grew in size beyond proportions as compared to actual need. The Committee encountered resistance in its effort to reorganize the organizations under review. There was no chain of command and no instruction manual in most of the organizations. Also records were not properly kept. Administrative and financial powers were concentrated at the top.

Significant Recommendations

The Committee's recommendations included:

> (a) preparation of organization charts, manuals, annual activity report; (b) setting up O&M units in bigger corporations; (c) delegation of more administrative and financial powers down the hierarchy; (d) timely release of funds from ministries; (e) promotion be based on merit and training to be availed by component officials, and (f) effectuation of revised organization charts (Report of MLC-II, 1984, pp. 14-16).

Outcome

Many of the recommendations of the Committee were accepted and implemented by the government after scrutiny. The implementation of MLC-II's recommendations led to reduction in the number of public statutory organizations (autonomous, semiautonomous bodies and allied organizations) from 155 to 109. The Committee's work resulted in identifying surplus manpower and consequently 28,740 posts were slashed. Organization charts for various organizations were also approved by the government in line with the recommendations of MLC-II.

COMMITTEE FOR EXAMINATION OF IRREGULARITIES (CEI)

A Committee for Examination of Irregularities in Appointment and Promotion of Officers and Staff in the Government (CEI) was constituted in September 1982 under the chairmanship of a Brigadier. The other members included a member of the Bangladesh Public Service Commission, a Joint Secretary, a Lieutenant-Colonel and a Deputy Secretary. The Deputy Secretary was designated as also the secretary to the Committee.

Mission

The Committee's tasks were:

a. to examine the irregularities committed in the appointment and promotion of officers and staff in various ministries/divisions/departments . . . and fix a deadline by which all recruitment rules are to be framed and notified;
b. to examine the circumstances in which ad-hoc appointments were continued . . . and recommend appropriate measures;
c. to examine the circumstances under which certain posts were taken out of the purview of the Bangladesh Public Service Commission (BPSC);
d. to examine the cases of unusual delay in implementing the recommendations of the BPSC regarding appointment;
e. to examine the system of encadrement of officers in different cadres of the BCS with a view to streamlining procedure; and
f. to suggest ways and means to streamline recruitment/promotion in various ministries/divisions /departments and development projects (Report of CEI, 1983, pp. 131-132).

Significant Recommendations

The CEI made as many as one hundred recommendations under fourteen headings. The major recommendations of the Committee included:

a. framing of new recruitment rules to regularize ad-hoc and irregular appointments and to avoid recurrence of irregularities in appointments and promotion;
b. framing of Seniority Rules and Gradation Lists of officials and staff;
c. constitution of Selection Committees and Departmental Promotion Committees in ministries/divisions, departments/directorates/ offices;
d. appointment and promotion to be made strictly in accordance with relevant rules and regulations;
e. ad-hoc appointments should be made when absolutely necessary for a limited period and regularized within that period;
f. the system of taking services and posts out of the purview of the Public Service Commission (PSC) should be resorted to in only very special circumstances;
g. ensuring that the recommendations of the PSC regarding appointment and promotion are implemented on time;
h. appointment under development projects be made strictly in accordance with recruitment rules;
i. recruitment to different cadres/sub-cadres of the Bangladesh Civil Service should be made strictly in accordance with the Bangladesh Recruitment Rules, 1981;
j. regularly appointed eligible officers should be encadred;
k. time scales of pay be given to all officers;
l. appointment and encadrement of officers in the Senior Services Pool should be made on the basis of selection by the PSC and the strengthening of PSC by appointment of more members (Report of CEI, 1983, pp. 1-18).

Outcome

The government did not show any enthusiasm for the recommendations of the Committee. The recommendations were not even discussed at higher levels in the hierarchy. Consequently, the recommendations of the CEI remained almost unnoticed and not implemented.

NATIONAL PAY COMMISSION (NPC-II)

A fifteen member National Pay Commission (NPC-II) was appointed in May 1984. The NPC-II was headed by a Justice of the Supreme Court. The membership of the Commission had full-time as well as part-time members. A former Vice Chancellor of the Bangladesh University of Engineering and Technology, a retired Secretary to the government, a former member of the Planning Commission and a senior civil servant were full-time members. The latter was to become the secretary to the NPC-II as well. Among the part-time members were a Secretary to the government, a retired Secretary, President of the Federation of the Chambers of Commerce and Industry, a chartered accountant, a professor of medicine of Dhaka Medical College, managing director of a commercial bank in the private sector, a retired educationist and former advisor to the government, a representative each of the Ministry of Finance and the University Grants Commission.

Mission

The NPC-II's responsibilities included:

a. to recommend suitable pay structure for officers and employees of government, semi-government and autonomous bodies;
b. to recommend other benefits including salaries, house rent, medical allowances, conveyance allowance or arrangements;
c. to formulate suitable principles for refixing salaries, allowances and retirement allowances from time to time considering changes in the price of commodities;
d. to recommend suitable retirement allowances for officers and employees (*The Bangladesh Observer*, 1 June 1984).

In making its recommendations the Commission was asked to take into consideration such variables as cost of living for a family of four, educational expenses of wards of officers and employees, sources of government revenue, need for attracting brilliant people in the administration, necessity for attracting individuals with professional expertise, need for increasing efficiency of officers and employees, and demand and supply of efficient persons in technical professions (*The Bangladesh Observer*, 1 June 1984).

Significant Recommendations

The NPC-II recommended the highest scale of taka 7500 and the lowest taka 660 in twenty grades along with the fringe benefits including the house rent, medical, conveyance, educational and festival allowances (Obaidullah, 1995, p. 151).

Outcome

The government accepted in principle the major recommendations of the Commission. But while implementing the NPC-II recommendations pertaining to pay scale the government made some modifications. The Modified New Scales of Pay (MNSP) which came into effect on June 1, 1985 was the result of NPC-II's recommendations. The MNSP fixed the lowest salary at taka 500 and highest at take 6000 with a defferential of 12:1 between the highest and the lowest pay (Obaidullah, 1995, p. 151).

NATIONAL PAY COMMISSION (NPC-III)

A National Pay Commission (NPC-III) was appointed in August, 1989. The Commission was headed by a former Secretary. A former ambassador, a retired Secretary, a senior army officer and a senior civil servant were members of NPC-III. The last member was designated to act as the secretary to the Commission in addition to his duty as a member.

Mission

The Commission's purview included all categories of public employees of the traditional public sector as well as autonomous organizations.

Outcome

The government accepted the Commission's recommendations and a Revised National Scale of Pay (RNSP) was announced in September 1991. The RNSP, which is still operational contains twenty scales of pay with taka 900 fixed as the minimum salary and taka 10,000 as the maximum salary per month (Bangladesh Gazette Extraordinary 14 September 1991). It has been observed that since Bangladesh's independence for the first time RNSP contained a revised pay scale which was at par with the then inflation rate to prevent standard of living from further erosion (Obaidullah, 1995, p.153).

It needs to be pointed out that though the government agreed on twenty scales of pay but NPC-III's recommendation relating to highest and lowest pay of taka 13000 and 1250 respectively was substantially moderated during implementation and resultant RNSP.

OTHER COMMITTEES

During Ershdad era, beside major committees and commissions as discussed earlier, a number of high-level committees and a cabinet sub-committee were constituted between 1985 and 1987 to review critical micro problems afflicting the functioning of the civil service. The membership of these committees were confined to cabinet ministers, top military brass and senior civil servants.

Secretaries Committee

The Secretaries Committee on Administrative Development (SCAD) was constituted on 20 April 1985 under the chairmanship of the Secretary, Cabinet Division, to solve critical problem of inadequate promotion prospect in various cadre services. The Committee recommended that status quo in those ten cadre services be maintained where promotion prospect had been satisfactory.

Special Committee

The Special Committee (SC) was appointed on 23 December 1985 to review the structure of the Senior Services Pool (SSP) and anomalies caused by its (SSP's) introduction. The Committee was headed by the Chief of Navy and the Deputy Chief Martial Law Administrator (DCMLA). The Committee's recommendations included: (a) continuation of SSP as a cadre; (b) entry into SSP at the level of Deputy Secretary only through examinations to be conducted by the Public Service Commission; (c) promotion within SSP would be strictly on the basis of merit; (d) members of technical cadres to be inducted into SSP on merit; and (e) tenure of secretaries be limited to eight years to ensure greater opportunities for promotion at higher levels of administration (Khan, 1994, p. 23).

Cabinet Sub-Committee

The Cabinet Sub-Committee was constituted on 3 June 1987 to examine the report of the Secretaries Committee and the Special Committee. The Sub-Committee was headed by the Deputy Prime Minister. Two senior cabinet ministers were members of the Committee. Initially, the Sub-Committee endorsed most of the recommendations of the Special Committee. It also made a number of recommendations including creation of 50% of posts of Deputy Secretaries and Senior Deputy Secretaries within the pay scale of taka 4200-5200 for making SSP more attractive and selection of Joint Secretaries by the Council Committee. The Sub-Committee opposed Special Committee's recommendations concerning fixation of tenure for Secretaries on the ground that it would be an unwise move.

Council Committee

The Council Committee on Senior Appointments and Services Structure considered reports of both the Special Committee and the Cabinet Sub-Committee on 31 October 1987 and upheld most of the recommendations of the former and a few of the latter. The Council Committee made a number of recommendations on its own. It's recommendations included continuation of SSP as a cadre; limiting entrance into SSP at the level of Deputy Secretary; and keeping secretaries tenure open.

But the recommendations of the Council Committee were not approved by the President. The President met several times with members of the Cabinet Sub-Committee. On the basis of such meetings the Cabinet Sub-Committee came up with a new set of recommendations which received presidential approval on 2 June 1989. The approved recommendation included: (a) abolition of the SSP; (b) filling up of posts of Deputy Secretaries and Joint Secretaries by promotion on the basis of quota reservation for various cadres ; and (c) no quota reservation for any cadre the posts of Additional Secretaries and Secretaries (Khan, 1994, pp. 24-35).

KHALEDA ZIA ERA: LACK OF COMMITMENT

Khaleda Zia, widow of late President Ziaur Rahman, became Prime Minister in March 1991 after her party Bangladesh Nationalist Party (BNP) won majority seats in the parliamentary elections held in that year under the supervision of a caretaker government. Khaleda Zia's five year rule was marked by constant confrontation with major opposition party the Awami League which ultimately resulted in all the opposition political parties boycott of the parliament during the last two years of her government.

Economic policies of her government were guided by the belief that deregulation and privatization would bring about prosperity. But the prosperity that resulted was confined to few politicians and businessmen who were connected with the ruling party. In the name of opening the economy opportunities were provided to fortunate few to plunder the national exchequer. One crisis after another in the economic arena made things difficult for the common people. The bureaucracy became a place where loyalty to the ruling party mattered in terms of posting, transfer and promotion especially at the higher echelon. A number of scandals became public in which a minister in-charge of the Establishment Ministry took bribes to the tune of crores in the name of giving promotions to officials. A number of senior ministers were involved in large-scale corruption. The civil servants lost faith in their political masters. They became dispirited, frustrated and disenchanted. Political victimization became prominent. There was no motivation for civil servants to put in their best.

Khaleda Zia was not interested in administrative reform. Consequently, there was no political commitment to bring about meaningful changes within the civil service. Only one reform committee was set up that even did not submit its recommendations during Khaleda Zia's tenure of office. Two cabinet sub-committees also delivered nothing in concrete terms.

ADMINISTRATIVE REORGANIZATION COMMITTEE E (ARC)

The ARC was appointed in August, 1993. The Committee consisted of six members including the chairman, all of them were senior civil servants either retired or serving. The junior-most member was designated as member-secretary to the Committee.

Mission

The ARC was asked to do the following:

> (i) to review the government's administrative structure and staffing patterns in ministries; (ii) to ascertain actual personnel need; and (iii) to make proposals for reorganizing the machinery of government to meet the new demands placed on the civil service (Khan, 1994: 25).

The Committee submitted its report to the government only recently after three time extension of its tenure. The recommendations of the ARC were finalized after conducting extensive surveys on functions, workloads, equipment, objective conditions, practical situation, economic resources and other relevant matters of public organizations (*The Independent*, 29 January 1996).

Significant Recommendations

The Committee made a number of recommendations that touched the public service, the judiciary and the legislature. The relevant recommendations are:

> (i) reduction of the number of ministries from present 35 to 22 and slashing of the number of administrative organizations from 257 to 224; (ii) abolition of 47 organizations and reduction of 43 others through merger or reorganization; (iii) provisional structure for the office of Ombudsman; (iv) reduction of the Planning Commission to a much slimmer body styled as the National Planning Organization to be responsible for enunciation of economic and development policies and formulation of national plan under the headship of a principal secretary; (v) renaming of the Ministry of Finance as the Ministry of Finance and Economy; (vi) creation of a Secretariat for the Supreme Court for handling all work arising out of the separation of the judiciary form the executive; (vii) separation of audit from accounts to save the government from being drowned with unresolved and unresolvable audit objections; (viii) provision for office assistance and small fund for all members of parliament; and (ix) reduction in the number of existing missions abroad (*The Independent*, 30 August 1996; *The Daily Star*, 30 August 1996).

The ARC members felt that if their recommendations were implemented a saving of taka 174 crore would result and 46,276 civil servants would become redundant. The government has not taken any decision as yet on the recommendations of the Committee. This is understandable as a new government under the leadership of the Awami League chairperson Sheikh Hasina has assumed power after the successful completion of the parliamentary elections in June 1996 held under the auspices of a caretaker government.

During the tenure of Khaleda Zia government two cabinet sub-committees were set up under the leadership of two senior cabinet ministers. One sub-committee looked as how to bring about efficiency in the civil service while the other considered ways and means to remove pay discrimination among members of cadre civil services and those who belonged to other civil services.

The first committee prepared a report while the second committee even did not do that. But the government neither did take any action on the report of the committee on efficiency nor made it available to the public. Deliberations of both the committees and their recommendations are not known.

SHEIKH HASINA ERA: AN UNCERTAIN BEGINNING

The leader of the Awami Leauge Sheikh Hasina's assumption of power in June 1996 after her party's victory in the parliamentary elections of 12 June 1996 marks the return of the Awami Leauge to power after a lapse of twenty-one years.

NATIONAL PAY COMMISSION-IV (NPC-IV)

Within two months of assuming office the new government announced the appointment of the National Pay Commission-IV (NPC-IV). The Commission consists of fifteen members including the chairman. Of the members three are full-timers and the rest are part-timers. The full-time members and the chairman are all retired senior civil servants.

The part-time members include an economist from the University of Dhaka, President of the Bangladesh Employers Association, a member of the Planning commission, a retired professor of Dhaka Medical College, a former chairman of Capital Development Authority, a former deputy governor of Bangladesh Bank, a well-known gynecologist, a representative of the army and a representative each from the Ministries of Industry, Law and Finance not below the rank of the Joint Secretary (*The Daily Janakantha*, 19 August 1996). A Joint Secretary of the Ministry of Finance will act as member-secretary to the Commission. Though all the full-time members are retired civil servants still some of the part-time members have been chosen from different professional and other groups. But it needs to be mentioned that all the representatives of three ministries and member-secretary are serving civil servants. So the civil servants -- retired and serving – have a comfortable majority in terms of membership of the Commission.

Mission

The NPC-IV has been asked to make recommendations on the following: (i) an appropriate pay structure for officials and employees; (ii) other facilities, i.e. house rent, medical treatment, transportation that are outside pay; (iii) an appropriate policy guideline for refixing pay allowances and pension of civil servants in view of changes in the prices of commodities; (iv) appropriate pension benefits for officials and employees; (v) developing standards to correctly evaluate performance of officials and employees in terms of giving them rewards and punishment; and (vi) inconsistencies in the pay structure (*The Daily Janakantha*, 19 August 1996).

In making their recommendations the Commission members will take into consider the following:

> (i) monthly expenditure of a family of four; (ii) educational expenses of two children; (iii) provisions for government taxes and revenue; and (iv) income and expenditure of different units and organizations of the government (*Dhaka Courier*, 30 August 1996).

Significant Recommendations

The Commission is yet to submit its recommendations to the government. But it has been learnt that the NPC-IV has recommended for 20 scales of pay with the lowest pay being Tk. 1800 and highest pay fixed at Tk. 18000. (*Daily Janakantha*, 21 April 1997). The Commission also suggested doubling of medical and conveyance allowances for all categories of all public servants. It has also been reported that the Ministry of Finance has decided to allocate Tk. 15000 crores in the next budget to meet the expenditure to be incurred in implementing the recommendations of the Commission (*Daily Janakantha*, 21 April 1997)

ADMINISTRATIVE REFORMS COMMISSION (ARC)

Only recently a seven-member Administrative Reforms Commission (ARC) has been constituted with a former Cabinent Secretary as its chairman. The membership of the Commission is dominated by the members of the erstwhile CSP. The chairman, the NGO representative, the political category's representative, the only permanent member all belonged to the erstwhile CSP. The member-secretary belongs to the BCS (Administration) cadre. The 'specialist' member, though is a faculty member in the Public Administration Department, University of Dhaka, is not a specialist in public sector reform. The composition of the Commission has already been criticized by professional associations and experts in the field as biased and ill-motivated. It is widely apprehended that the present composition of the Commission will frustrate and derail the present government's attempt to reform and revitalize the public service. There is still time for the government to thoroughly recast the Commission's membership by dropping all the members including the chairman and inducting relevant individuals from the NGO, academia, professional groups, private sector and the civil service.

Mission

The terms of reference of the Commission are:

(a) Examine and identify implementable recommendations of:
 – Public Administration Efficiency Study, 1989
 – Public Administration Sector Study, 1993
 – Towards Better Government in Bangladesh, 1993
 – Government That Works : Reforming Public Sector, 1996 ;

(b) Recommend measures for improving the quality and standard of service, achieve transparency and efficiency;

(c) Recommend steps towards rightsizing the government and determine the scope and nature of its activities;

(d) Examine the organization and structure of civil services and the system of incentives now prevalent and recommend measures to make it more effective and dynamic, suited to the needs of time;

(e) Make recommendations for necessary legal and procedural changes;
(f) Recommend measures for administrative decentralization and reorganization of local government structure;
(g) Recommend steps to curb corruption in public service;
(h) Recommend measures for strengthening parliamentary vigilance over various functions of government;
(i) Recommend measures for creation of awareness for effecting economy in public expenditure, ensuring value for money and improved quality of service.

The Commission may, from time to time, submit its recommendations spelling out financial implications as well as the mode of implementation.

The terms of reference (TOR) of the Commission is two broad. It appears everything under the sun falls within its purview. Taking into consideration the composition of ARC one wonders whether it can even act as a recommendatory body let alone perform such other crucial functions of supervisory or monitoring in terms of implementable recommendations of the body. Recently the chairman of ARC submitted his resignation to the government on the ground that he did not receive any cooperation from civil servants in performing his duties. The government has already accepted his resignation. But his successor is yet to be appointed. Another member of the Commission has also resigned. Also there is growing disenchantment with the performance of the expert member and her credibility is rather low among other members of the Commission. The Commission has so far held two meeting with very little result. It is understood that the Commission will not be able to fulfill its mandate.

CONCLUSION

Bangladesh's failed experience in implementation of major administrative reform measures can be explained if one looks at a number of factors. The factors are examined below.

First, political commitment, a pre-condition for successful implementation of reforms, has been missing. Successive governments have only given lip service to the call for overhauling the civil bureaucracy. Governments have been unwilling to pay the price for civil service reform. Rather the intention has been to placate and appease all segments and factions within the civil service. The social, political and economic costs of keeping a hide-bound and inefficient bureaucracy has not been understood. Donor pressure forced governments to promise reforms that would not be kept. Some governments played the 'reform game' by appointing committees and commissions whose recommendations they had no intention to accept let alone implement. The motive was to gain political mileage with the public at least for the time being. But the people saw acts like this too many times before to believe that things would change for the better. In spite of numerous public utterances by political leaders in power people saw no reform forthcoming. Major administrative reforms became hostage to political opportunism and lack of foresight on the part of political leaders.

Second, bureaucratic resistance to reform is too well-known. Civil servants, specially the ones occupying senior positions, have been unwilling to reform themselves. The reform implementation committees under their leadership had to fail. Also bureaucratic domination -- both civil and military -- of the membership of the committees and commissions pre-determined recommendations of most of the reform bodies. These bodies failed to come up with farreaching and future-oriented recommendations. The chairman and members of such committees and commissions were interested to maintain the status quo only. Recommendations were intended to adjust with the present and not to face challenges that lay ahead. Explanations were always ready as to why changes could not even be considered. Incrementalist approach became the order of the day. Modifications, not changes, were preferred and recommended. Maintenance of the status quo became the paramount goal of the bureaucracy.

Third, the mission of some of the committees and commissions were too broad. They were supposed to study everything and recommend about everything. That was not to happen. Time constraint, lack of professional staff and logistical support, infrequent holding of meetings all in varying degrees affected the quality as well as the timely presentation of reform bodies findings and recommendations. Naturally, missions of committees and commissions remained ideals that could not even be reached.

Fourth, reform implementation committees were exclusively manned by bureaucrats – civil and military. Their deliberations suffered from the tendency to preserve narrow sectarian interests. Naturally, public interest was forgotten. Recommendations of reform bodies were probed, dissected by implementation committees and sometimes implemented by the government in disjointed manner at irregular intervals thereby negating the intended benefits of such recommendations. Advice and suggestions from professionals were never sought in the reform implementation process. Reliance on the ability and good intention of civil and military officers was the only course of action that remained open. But that proved to be more illusory than real.

Fifth, though there has been public discontent about the poor quality of the public service and dissatisfaction on the part of citizens about the behavioural patterns of public servants demonstrated in public administrator-citizen contact surprisingly very few initiatives been taken to organize citizens to reform the civil service. No attempt has been made to form public interest groups to campaign on specific issues like accountability, transparency, efficiency and productivity in the civil service. One of the consequences of such a situation has been the lack of representation of citizens in either reform bodies or reform implementation bodies. The non-governmental organizations (NGOs) have not been able to play their due role in mobilizing citizens against inefficient public services and excesses of public servants. The role of the press has also been rather inconsequential. The tendency of the press has been to highlight mismanagement and corruption in public service mostly at the lower level of the bureaucracy. Occasionally, lapses of senior civil servants are reported without disclosing their identities. Investigative reporting in terms of coverage and quality has improved in recent years. But desirable stage is yet to be attained. The role of the press in educating the public about the happenings within the public service has not been satisfactory. But the failure of the press is most glaring when it comes to prepare the citizens as how to cope with and change the public service. It is in the area of providing direction to the citizens that the press has failed most. One of the reasons for such a failure has been the continuing dependence of the press on government advertisement and supply of newsprint at a subsidized rate. It is well known that civil servants play crucial role in giving advertisements and ensuring supply of newsprint without these many newspapers will face closure.

It will appear from the discussions above that both the political and bureaucratic elite deliberately and purposively opposed implementation of major administrative reforms. For them change is a frightening prospect. They are comfortable to work with a system that they have inherited. They are unwilling to experiment with new ideas, new methods and new structures even when such changes are badly needed. Citizens failure to organize as effective public interest groups as well as ineffective role of the press to act as harbinger of mass awareness also significantly contributed to the failure of major administrative reform measures in the civil service in Bangladesh.

REFERENCES

Bangladesh Observer, *The* (1984). An English daily newspaper, 1 June.

Daily Star, The (1996). An English daily newspaper, 30 August.

Dhaka Courier, The (1996). An English newsweekly, 30 August

GOPRB (1972). *Report of the Civil Administration Restoration Committee*. Part 1, January. Dhaka : Government of the People's Republic of Bangladesh (GOPRB).

GOPRB (1973).*Report of the Administrative and Services Reorganization Committee.* Part 1, *The Services*, April, Dhaka: GOPRB.

GOPRB (1975). *Report of the Administrative and Services Reorganization Committee*. Part V: *Summary of Recommendations.* May, Dhaka: GOPRB.

GOPRB (1973).*Report of the National Pay Commission: Bangladesh.*

Volume 1: *Main Text*, May, Dhaka: GOPRB.

GOPRB (1977). *Report of the Pay and Services Commission: Bangladesh*. Part 1: *The Services*, Volume 1, May, Dhaka : GOPRB.

GOPRB (1982).*Report of the Martial Law Committee for Examining Organizational Set Up of Ministries/Divisions, Departments, Directorates and Other Organizations Under Them*. Phase 1, May, Dhaka: GOPRB.

GOPRB (1983). *Report of the Committee for Examination of Irregularities in Appointment and Promotion of Officers and Staff in the Government*. April, Dhaka: GOPRB.

GOPRB (1984). *Report of the Martial Law Committee for Examining Organizational Set Up of Public Statutory Corporations (Autonomous/Semi-Autonomous Bodies and Allied Organizations)*. February, Dhaka: GOPRB.

GOPRB (1991). *Bangladesh Gazzette Extraordinary*. September, Dhaka: GOPRB.

Independent, The (1996). An English daily newspaper, 29 January.

Independent, The (1996). An English daily newspaper, 30 August.

Janakantha, The (1993). A vernacular daily newspaper, 19 August.

Khan, M. M. (1991). *Politics of Administrative Reforms: A Case Study of Bangladesh*. New Delhi: Ashish Publishing House.

Khan, M. M. (1993). *Civil Service Management in Bangladesh*. Dhaka: United Nations Development Programme (UNDP)

Khan, M. M. (1994). *Civil Service Reform in Bangladesh: An Agenda for Change*. Dhaka: The World Bank.

Khan, M. M. (1997). "Resistance to Administrative Modernization in Bangladesh" in Classie, A. and Meininger, M-C. eds. *Administrative Modernization*. Brussels: International Institute of Administrative Sciences.

Khan, M. M. and Zafarullah, H.M. (1982). "Administrative Reform and Bureaucratic Intransigence in Bangladesh" in Caiden, G.E. and Siedentopf, H. eds. *Strategies for Administrative Reform*. Lexington, Mass.: Lexington/D.C. Heath Company, pp. 139-151.

Obaidullah, A.T.M. (1995). "Reorganization of Pay Policy and Structure in Bangladesh: The Quest for Living Wage", *Journal of the Asiatic Society of Bangladesh* 40(1): 135-156.

CHAPTER 6

Major Administrative Reforms and Role of International Donors in Bangladesh

INTRODUCTION

Research studies (Sobhan 1982; Sobhan and Bhattacharya, 1990) have shown the nature and extent of influence of international donors in the economy of Bangladesh. International donors provide economic and technical assistance (TA) which together constitute foreign development aid to this country. It is through this foreign aid that the international donors significantly influence the public policy making process in Bangladesh.

Technical Assistance (TA) is the key component of foreign aid. The TA usually takes three forms (Gant, 1979:287). These are: (a) expert personnel to fill the gaps in host country's complement of trained manpower; (b) training of such staff to make up the deficiency; and (c) institution building to create the agency and system capacity of a country to meet its requirements for technology, expertise and specialized personnel.

The focus of this chapter is on the role of four international donors in the area of civil service reform in Bangladesh. Of the four donors, three, the International Bank for Reconstruction and Development (IBRD), the United Nations Development Programme (UNDP), the United States Agency for International Development (USAID) provided research and advisory services, training facilities and supplied equipment and all these are considered objectives of TA programmes while the involvement of the fourth one, i.e. the Overseas Development Authority (ODA) has not been as extensive as the other three. More specifically, the present chapter examines the recommendations of donor-sponsored bodies and analyses responses of successive governments to donor-driven reform initiatives.

ROLE OF INTERNATIONAL DONORS IN ADMINISTRATIVE REFORM

The involvement of international donors in reforming the civil service system in Bangladesh began in late 1970s. All four international donors, the IBRD, the UNDP, the USAID and the ODA of UK have invested together considerable resources to bring about efficiency, productivity, effectiveness and accountability in the civil service.

TRAINING NEEDS SURVEY (TNS)

In 1979, IBRD hired a political scientist of Bangladeshi origin settled in USA to conduct a training needs survey of three major public sector training institutions. The expatriate consult with the assistance of a Bangladeshi public administration specialist studied the functions of three erstwhile training institutes, i.e. Bangladesh Administrative Staff College (BASC), National Institute of Public Administration (NIPA) and Civil Officer's Training Academy (COTA) to assess the training needs of class I gazetted officers vis-a-vis the capabilities of the institutions.

The Training Needs Survey (TNS) was intended to be a preamble to the government's preparation of a training plan and formulation of a training policy.

After seventeen years of the submission of the short-term consultancy report the government has neither the training plan nor an official training policy. This is strange because the Zia government as early as 20 January 1981 established a National Training Council (NTC). One of the major responsibilities of the NTC was to formulate a National Training Policy (NTP) and review it from time to time in terms of felt needs and changed priorities

(Khan, 1984). A document titled Training Policy for Government Officials was prepared in draft form single-handedly by the Additional Secretary of the Ministry of Establishment (MOE) without consulting other members of the NTC (Khan, 1986). But this document never received formal approval by the government of the day and the situation has not changed since then.

PRE-INVESTMENT STUDY FOR A PUBLIC ADMINISTRATION TRAINING AND MANAGEMENT IMPROVEMENT PROJECT (PATMIP) IN BANGLADESH

The UNDP's involvement in civil service reform began in 1980 with financing of the Pre-Investment Study for a Public Administration Training and Management Improvement Project (PATMIP) in Bangladesh. The Study was managed and supervised by the IBRD and conducted by the Institute of Public Administration (IPA) of New York, USA. The Study's cost amounted to US $250,000.

The Study was carried out by a team of expatriate consultants. They were aided by some local consultants. The Study Team worked for almost four months in two phases between November and December 1980 and January and April 1981 and produced two reports, i.e. an inception report and a final report.

The Study's main responsibility was to prepare a project for possible IDA financing. The proposed project was to: (a) improve public administration through Bangladesh Public Administration Training Centre (BPATC) and Staff Training Institute (STI); (b) strengthen management functions, standards and procedures used by the Organization and Management (O&M) Wing of the Ministry of Establishment (MOE); (c) strengthen the Training and Career Planning Wing (TCPW) of MOE; and (d) review personnel management aspect of public administration in Bangladesh (IPA, 1981:11).

The Study's observations and recommendations for a technical assistance project concentrated on three areas: (a) training - management and administrative, (b) personnel management and (c) O&M services.

In the area of training, the Study found the following deficiencies: (a) little attention given to training needs of officials at the intermediate and lower levels; (b) missions of the National Institute of Public Administration (NIPA) and the Bangladesh Administrative Staff College (BASC) -- two erstwhile institutes of training for mid-and higher-level civil servants and since then merged into BPATC --lacked definition and clear purpose; (c) lack of rationalization in the functions and responsibilities of the STI -- a training institute that imparted training to non-gazetted staff and now merged with four Regional Public Administration Training Centers (RPATCs); (d) in-house and on-the-job training not been fully utilized; (e) quality of training been generally low; and (f) status and career prospect of staff engaged in training been undesirable (IPA, 1981:6).

Accordingly, the Study recommended (a) redressing the training needs of public officials working at intermediate and lower levels; (b) purposes of NIPA and BASC needed to be studied and redefined; (c) upgrading of the status of STI and rationalization of its functions; (d) full and systematic exploitation of in-house and on-the-job training capacities; (e) establishment of a new Training Wing in MOE and small Training Cells (TCs) in all major ministries to encourage and foster greater departmental involvement in training programmes; and (f) setting up of a Training of Trainer's (TOT) Institute within BPATC to enhance quality of training instruction (IPA, 1981:6-7).

In the area of personnel management, a seven-point action plan was recommended. These included: (a) establishment of a Central Personnel Office (CPO) for developing, coordinating and administering government- wide policies; (b) preparation of a Government Personnel Manual for codification of personnel policies, rules and procedures as a basis for operation of a decentralized personnel management system administered through personnel officers in respective ministries; (c) establishment of a government-wide job analysis programme; (e) setting up of a system of performance evaluation; (e) development of an open system of career advancement; (f) creation of a manpower planning system; and (g) development of a comprehensive personnel record system (IPA, 1981:7-8).

In the area of O&M, the Study focused attention to major weakness in the organizational structure of the civil service system in Bangladesh -- the physical and organizational separation of policy making, i.e. ministries located in the secretariat and execution of such policies, i.e. in attached departments (IPA, 1981:8).

The recommendations of the Study in the O&M area included : establishment of a Central Management Services Division (CMSD) within MOE as a centre of initiative and innovation in all matters pertaining to managerial and administrative efficiency (IPA, 1981:9).

One of the major outcomes of the Study was the merger of BASC, NIPA and COTA and their co-location in Savar within the framework of BPATC and upgradation of the status of STI and placing its functions and responsibilities to four RPACs. Also a Training Wing within MOE was created and placed under the jurisdiction of the Additional Secretary. An Establishment Manual in two volumes was prepared in 1988 by the O & M Wing of the MOE but not in the way the Study recommended. But the volumes are in any case now dated.

But the most of important recommendations were not implemented by the government. These included: (a) establishing a Central Personnel Office (CPO), a government- wide job analysis programme, a system of performance evaluation; (b) creation of a manpower planning system; (c) development of a comprehensive personnel record system; (d) setting up of a TOT institute and TCs in large ministries; (e) establishment of Central Management Services Division (CMSD); and (f) development of an open system of career advancement.

PUBLIC ADMINISTRATION PROJECT (PAP)

Public Administration (Training, Personnel and Management) Project (PAP) funded by the World Bank lasted seven years, i. e. 1983-1990 and its cost amounted to US $ 14.71 million. The PAP was designed to enhance efficiency in the civil service through improved and expanded training, upgraded personnel management and better organization and management (O&M).

The Project was the outcome of IBRD's continuous effort to upgrade public service system in Bangladesh. The IBRD set a number of conditions before offering to finance the Project. First, it wanted the government to prepare a broad-based training plan for civil service along with a detailed statement about the training policy. Second, it asked for the delineation in the clear-cut manner the role of existing training institutions in the public sector. Third, it envisaged undertaking of investigation about the need for and the means and costs of improving public administration training and management standards and procedures.

The government did not prepare a training plan. The training policy was not formulated as indicated earlier. But the government clarified the role of the training institutions. The government also agreed to undertake a diagnostic study, i.e. PATMIP, discussed in the earlier section.

The major focus of the Project was to enhance the capacity of the Bangladesh Public Administration Training Centre (BPATC) and the Ministry of Establishment (MOE) (Staff Appraisal Report, 1983: 16). In the case of BPATC the capacity enhancement would include such measures as: (a) increasing its enrolment capacity; and (b) upgrading its quality of training. Strengthening of MOE would be done by: (a) developing and instituting a modernized Personnel Management Information System (PMIS) and (b) establishing a Management Services Wing (MSW).

The Project was to assist the government to: (a) expand the physical capacity of the BPATC through construction and equipping of teaching facilities, library, administrative buildings and a dormitory; (b) improve the quality of training at BPATC through providing fellowships and special training courses to upgrade the teaching staff, increasing the relevance of curricula to training needs with the assistance of experts, developing a programme of research and case studies and upgrading equipment and training material; (c) enhance the present system of personnel administration though the introduction of a modern PMIS with the assistance of experts and reinforced by staff training and additional equipment and salary support for incremental staff; (d) strengthen administrative systems and procedures through the financing of experts, staff training, equipment and incremental salaries to enhance the scope of the O&M Wing at MOE; and (e) upgrade project management capability in the MOE through provision of staff training, equipment and incremental staff salaries for the Project Implementation Wing (PIW) (Staff Appraisal Report, 1983: 17).

The training objective of the Project was substantially achieved. Buildings were constructed for housing, office and training purposes. A number of trainers were sent abroad to pursue higher studies and training in relevant disciplines and areas. A number of expatriate consultants were hired for curriculum development. But unpredictable political changes, rigid project design and management problems contributed to undue delays in achieving the physical and quality objectives of the training component (World Bank, 1993: 2).

In the case of the MOE, the impact of the Project was insignificant. Though both expatriate and local experts worked laboriously for months on the PMIS it was not introduced in the way specified in the project document. The MOE has a computerized information retrieval system. But that is neither comprehensive nor efficient. This is known as the Personnel Data Statement (PDS). The PDS contains information about officials belonging to only one cadre, i.e. the BCS (Administration). Also the capacity of the O&M Wing has not been increased to any significant degree as envisaged in the Project document. Also administrative procedures and systems have not been rationalized. The project management capacity of the MOE remains highly suspect.

It can be said that neither the PMIS nor the MSW objectives nor other planned improvements in the MOE such as strengthening its capacity to offer management services to other departments within were fully achieved because there was insufficient support and commitment, evidenced by constant changes of personnel and internal conflict over project management (World Bank, 1993:2).

MOBILIZATION AND MANAGEMENT OF PUBLIC RESOURCES (MMPR) IN BANGLADESH

An expatriate consultant under UNDP's Management Development Programme (MDP) prepared a preliminary report titled Mobilization and Management of Public Resources (MMPR) in Bangladesh: A Role for UNDP's MDP. The Report was outcome of the Consultant's seven week stay in Bangladesh, i.e. from April to June 1989.

The discussion which follows is confined to the Report's section on the civil service. Beside the civil service the other contents of the Report included deficiencies in public expenditure planning and budgeting and accounting, need for public resource mobilization and further decentralization.

The Report pointed out a number of deficiencies in the civil service system in Bangladesh. First, no single institution was responsible for civil service reform. Second, existence of fragmentation of authority was clearly noticeable resulting in lack of coordination between different agencies responsible for recruitment, training and promotion of civil servants. Third, civil service policies were not based on adequate research. Fourth, long-term impact of rules and procedures on the functioning of the civil service was not given careful attention. Fifth, training rules and regulations had not been embodied in any coherent policy framework. Sixth, the BPATC's effectiveness as the apex training institution had been seriously undermined due to the simultaneous presence of a number of factors including deterioration in the quality of its instruction; under-utilization of library and other facilities; serious procurement irregularities; lack of relevant qualifications on the part of the faculty to undertake action-oriented research and consultancy; unhappiness of senior deputationist civil servants with their posting at Savar (location of BPATC outside the capital city) and harbouring a feeling of being dumped; directly-recruited junior faculty not adequately prepared to write case studies on real life situations due to lack of administrative experience at field and headquarters levels (Thomas, 1989 : 25 - 27).

The major recommendation of the Report was commissioning of a detail survey under the auspices of the MOE for preparation of career development plans for all civil servants and linking that with their training needs (Thomas, 1989:37). But this recommendation did not receive any attention from concerned government institutions.

PUBLIC ADMINISTRATION EFFICIENCY STUDY (PAES)

The Public Administration Efficiency Study (PAES) was undertaken at the request of the Bangladesh government and funded by the USAID. The Study was conducted by a team of local and expatriate consultants under the leadership of a Bangladeshi public administration scholar of international repute. The duration of the Study was six months, i.e. from May 1989 to November 1989.

The PAES consultant team had to work under the overall guidance and direction of the Steering Committee and direct supervision of four Working Groups. The Steering Committee was chaired by a senior minister and met every month to review the progress of work. Excepting one member beside the chairman the other eight members were all career civil servants. The Working Groups were led by civil servants and all other members of these groups belonged to the civil service. The consultants had to report to their respective working groups every two weeks. The nature of control exercised can be gauged from the fact that the consultants, against their best professional judgment, had to substantially alter and modify their draft reports to make them acceptable to members of the Steering Committee and the Working Groups. The Project Director and the Team Leader of the PAES Study kept the USAID informed of this development. The PAES had two broad objectives: (a) to suggest ways and means to make administration accountable and efficient; and (b) to recommend measures to make administration dynamic (Khan et al., 1989:1). The scope of the Study included six ministries, i.e., Establishment, Finance, Planning, Agriculture, Commerce, Industries and Irrigation, Water Development and Flood Control.

The focus of the Study was in four areas: (a) Secretariat System and Work Procedure; (b) Ministry-Department Relationships,

(c) Ministry-Corporation Relationships, and (d) Project Cycle Policies and Procedures. Within the above four areas, the Study's recommendations related to: (a) higher standards in administrative performance; (b) sound policy analysis; (c) implementation of policy and it's strategic implications; (d) delegation of authority for non-policymaking decisions; (e) procedures for staffing selected ministries/divisions; and (f) development and improvement of training facilities for development administration (Khan et al., 1989:6).

The five volume report of the PAES contained two hundred and four recommendations to overcome constraints to efficiency in the civil service.

The Study identified five major constraints to efficiency. These were: (a) diluted accountability; (b) overcentralization; (c) complex operating procedures; (d) weak support systems; and (f) inadequate human resources (Khan et al., 1989:1-3).

The significant recommendations of the Study included: (a) strengthening supervision through training and management support, (b) reducing secretariat's operational activities through delegation of routine personnel and financial matters to departments, corporations and subordinate offices; (c) reducing layers in decision making and encouraging horizontal communication between concerned officers and organizations; (d) enhancing O&M capacity to improve work procedures and organizational effectiveness; (e) modernization of office equipment; (f) introduction of a two-tier career system to raise quality of the senior civil service; (g) increasing incentives for high performance including wider use of merit as a criteria for promotion; (h) reducing staff rotation by extending posting period to five years in allied functional areas; (i) expanding practical, problem-solving training based on assessment of organizational needs; (j) providing better incentives to attract quality trainers; and (k) providing appropriate compensation structure for public corporation officials and employees (Khan et al., 1989:1-3).

The Study Team urged the government to take immediate actions to facilitate the implementation of the recommendations made. The steps suggested by the Study included: (a) providing high-level political support on a continuous basis for enhancing administrative efficiency in order to build a dynamic administration; (b) creation of a strong implementation committee; (c) implementation of existing government directives that would contribute to improved performance; (d) delegation of broader authority to implementing agencies; and (e) strengthening of accountability mechanisms (Khan et al., 1989:3)

The PAES also suggested that its recommendations in certain aspects be implemented on a pilot basis in selected ministries, departments, corporations and projects once the above-mentioned steps had been taken. These aspects included: (a) implementation strategies for improving human resources available to the government; (b) strengthening the problem solving capacity of the O&M Wing; (c) modernizing office systems; (d) simplifying procurement procedures; (e) improving auditing systems; and (f) strengthening project planning, implementation and monitoring systems (Khan et al., 1989:3).

The Ershad government did not take any action on the PAES Report till its fall in December 1990. The Caretaker Government of Justice Shabuddin Ahmed appointed on 26 February 1991 a Committee composed of seven senior civil servants under the chairmanship of the Additional Secretary, MOE to examine and analyse the recommendations of PAES Report and earmark which of its recommendations were implementable. The Committee submitted its recommendations on 30 June 1991. The Committee felt that a number of recommendations of PAES could be implemented without further delay as these would not require any change in the existing rules and regulations and not result in additional allocation of resources. The other recommendations could not be implemented without prior changes in the rules and regulations and involving extra expenses. The Khaleda Zia government appointed a Cabinet Sub-Committee headed by a minister to further examine the Committee's recommendations. The Cabinet approved implementation of PAES recommendations on 30 March 1992 with the stipulation that those recommendations that would require major structural changes and involve additional financial resources be referred back to it for decision.

On 23 July 1992 an inter-ministerial committee was formed headed by the Secretary, MOE to (a) monitor implementation of recommendations in different ministries/divisions; and (b) suggest ways to remove bottlenecks in the way of implementation. The last meeting of this Committee was held on 18 April 1993.

Other MOE actions included: (a) circulation of PAES report along with the review report to all ministries ; (b) asking other ministries/divisions monthly progress on the state of implementation of agreed upon recommendations; and (c) establishment of a work study unit in the MOE and twenty-nine ministries/divisions but effectiveness of a such a unit is yet to be tested.

Relatively slow progress in implementation of PAES recommendations has been mostly due to: (a) enormity and complexity of the task involved; (b) poor manpower and insufficient financial resources available at the MOE; (c) presence of strong bureaucratic inertia; and (d) lack of trust among civil servants as to the commitment of the government to carry reform measures to their logical conclusion. All these created a situation where civil servants found it convenient to adopt a combination of incremental and muddle through approaches where less controversial and minor recommendations like meeting procedures and filing systems were selectively taken up for implementation. But such implementation strategy had no impact on the civil service performance and efficiency.

Public Administration Sector Study in Bangladesh (PASSB)

The Public Administration Sector Study in Bangladesh (PASSB) was prepared by a team of international and local experts. The study period was six months, i.e. from February 1993 to July 1993. Five key areas were analysed on this basis of primary data. These were:(a) organization and structure of government; (b) civil service management; (c) performance and accountability; (d) decision making issues; (e) human resource development, education and training. Three contextual factors were also studied. They included: (a) administrative culture and norms; (b) policy development and analysis capacity; and (c) administrative challenges arising from the evolving context of government. Also reform implementation was identified as one of the important issues.

The major findings of the Study included: (a) poor performance due to apathy, narrow vision, a lack of commitment and inexperience of civil servants in operating within a democratic system of government; (b) parliamentary committees' ineffectiveness in holding ministries accountable to the parliament; (c) functioning of the secretariat suffers from the risk aversion, interference of politicians and senior officials and lack of data; (d) lack of clarity about the allocation of responsibilities between ministers and civil servants; (e) inefficient distribution of government responsibilities among too many ministries and divisions; (f) slow and complex decision making process; (g) inter-service tensions a feature of relations between cadres, between different batches and between class I officers and others; (h) general dissatisfaction with promotion and transfer; (i) deterioration in the level of education of recruits to the civil service; and (j) inadequacies in all types of training (UNDP, 1993 : 98-102).

The Study made fifty-two recommendations. The recommendations were organized into two groups, i.e. consolidation and reform proposals. Consolidation measures required immediate remedial actions while reform measures were intended to develop a more responsive, transparent and accountable civil service system.

The major recommendations of the Study included: (a) establishing results-oriented management systems through setting of objectives and measures of outputs and impacts throughout the government; (b) establishing units in each ministry and division, responsible for developing and applying performance criteria and measure and developing internal performance audit capability; (c) rationalizing government structure following examination of functions and need to improve coordination and to reduce number of ministries and divisions to make government more manageable; (d) systematically review and streamline government rules and regulations to eliminate red tape and redundant functions; (e) selection and promotion of officers be based on merit within a transparent process; (f) strengthening Public Service Commission; (g) decentralization of implementation of personnel policies to ministries and divisions; (h) replacing cadre and class system with personnel management system based on position classification and grades, for transparent, fair and efficient management of civil servants in a democratically responsive civil service; (i) understanding on a regular and systematic basis training needs assessment; (j) providing professional development opportunities for individual officers; and (k) appointment of reform implementation commission (UNDP, 1993: 103-110).

The government appointed an Advisory Committee in July 1993 under the chairmanship of the State Minister for Establishment to review the recommendations of PASSB. The other members of the Committee included seven secretaries, other officers and members of parliament. But from the very beginning senior civil servants were skeptic about the recommendations of PASSB. They felt that the recommendations were nebulous and insufficiently specific and had misgivings about ownership of the recommendations. The Advisory Committee was invited by the consultants to react to the findings of the Study before the report was finalized. But the members refused the offer on the ground that it would be a futile exercise without first having the draft report. On 2 August 1993 the report was presented to the government and its recommendations appeared in press simultaneously creating a sense of panic and anger among senior civil servants. So far the Advisory Committee has done nothing about implementation of PASSB.

Towards Better Government in Bangladesh (TBGB)

The Towards Better Government in Bangladesh (TBGB) Report was the outcome of a three week visit to UK, in June 1993 by four Secretaries of the government of Bangladesh under the sponsorship of Overseas Development Authority (ODA).

The TBGB Report made sixty-eight recommendations within six thematic areas covering the entire gamut of the civil service as well as the government. There were both short-term as well as long-term reform measures. The major recommendations of the TBGB included: (a) revision in the quota (reservation) system for recruitment of civil servants and enhancing the merit percentage from existing 45% to 60%; (b) promotion in the civil service be based on merit as demonstrated by performance in appropriate examinations and evaluation based on revised and transparent ACR; (c) three times failure in promotion examinations would compel civil servants to retire from service; (d) instituting a workable predetermined and transparent standard for efficient and speedy system of delivery of essential services; (e) linking standards of performance to a reward and penalty system; (f) installation of an efficiency unit in the cabinet division to monitor achievement of government-wide targets against standards of performance; (g) maximum use of market and price mechanisms inside the public sector to maximize efficiency and economy, to protect consumers who pay for services rendered by some units of the government; (h) evaluation of performance of public sector training institutions under a technical assistance project and review of training policy; and (i) combating corruption through updating necessary laws, appointing special judges, full use of Anti-Corruption Bureau's resources and revival of Anti-Corruption Council to scrutinize all cases against senior civil servants (Rahman et al., 1993: 90-98).

The TBGB Report also did not receive enthusiastic support from the BNP government. No attempt was made to seriously review its recommendations. Rather a ministerial level committee headed by the then communication minister was asked to look at it. But this committee even failed to produce a cursory report on the suitability of TBGB Report pertaining to the civil service system in Bangladesh.

Government That Works: Reforming the Public Sector (RPS)

The RPS Study was sponsored and financed by the World Bank. The Study was conducted between 1994 and 1995 at different phases. The Staff of the World Bank, Bangladeshi experts and some foreign consultants jointly prepared the Study. The Study pointed out a number of negative aspects of public sector in Bangladesh. These included: (i) a state apparatus which extends beyond the core functions of the state; (ii) a disabled economic environment with an intricate web of discretionary and disruptive regulations; (iii) a non-transparent system which is replete with unpredictable and surreptitious decision making on policy and operational aspects, and weak accountability; (iv) an oversized, complex and nearly unmanageable bureaucracy and institutional apparatus; (v) demotivated underpaid public employees at the senior and mid-management levels; (vi) an adversarial relationship between the public and private sectors, contributing both to a loss of credibility of public sector institutions and to obstacles to private sector growth; and (vii) overmanned SOEs with powerful public sector labour unions which have stymied efforts to reduce the massive losses by public enterprises, improve the efficiency of their operations or privatize them (World Bank, 1996a:11).

The massive indictment of the World Bank Report of the public sector in Bangladesh needs to be understood in the context of dwindling, inadequate and poor quality of services delivered to the people.

The main thrust of the Report is on delineating the core functions of the government and essential services to be provided to citizens. The Report points to a number of initiatives that need to be coordinated to overcome the wide-ranging deficiencies afflicting the public sector. These include:

(i) Redefining frontiers of public sector which means rightsizing the central government, enlarging the role of non-government organizations, local government and the private sector.
(ii) Enhancing level and nature of accountability and responsiveness of public organizations to their owners, i.e. parliament, citizens and consumers.
(iii) Streamlining regulations, laws and processes to ensure transparency, fairness and automacity of legal and regulatory institutions, policies and practices.
(iv) Overhauling rules and processes by which government conducts its policy and decision making functions.
(v) Maintaining an efficient, committed and professional public service,

without which government can neither be efficient nor responsive (World Bank, 1996a: xvi).

The Study underscored the difficulty of implementing major administrative reforms. But it warned that the 'cost of doing nothing will be lower growth, continued poverty and citizens continuing to receive less for more' (World Bank, 1996a: xix). Reforming the machinery of government must be viewed as a long drawn out process which needs more than anything else 'unequivocal and sustained commitment of political leadership to a less intrusive and more efficient government' (World Bank, 1996a: xix). Though political vision and mandate are crucial still the experience of other countries which have been successful in reforming their public sector indicates the importance of two levers of change. First, high-powered and professionally staffed institutional mechanisms must be in place to engender reforms, i.e. to design reforms, to operationalize them and monitor their implementation at every stage. Second, sound budget process is advocated to discipline the quality and direction of public expenditure policy.

The Study Report was released in March 1996 to selected individuals only. It has already been presented formally to the government.

CONCLUSION

There is a clear understanding among the donor community that the civil service in particular and the public sector in general due to structural, procedural and related deficiencies is completely out of pace with the reality as it obtains in Bangladesh. All the donor-sponsored studies pointed out in greater detail the fundamental and debilitating malices which have contributed to inefficiency, waste, low morale and corruption in the public sector. Naturally, the changes suggested by the reform bodies are essentially intended to transform the nature and character of the public sector. Mechanisms and strategies have also been recommended to operationalize and mange wide-ranging changes.

Not unexpectedly, the response from the government to donor initiatives has been lukewarm. Nothing much has happened. The intention is clear -- not to change as long as possible and to provide excesses as to why change is not feasible now.

The international donors have had almost no success in convincing the successive governments from that of General Ziaur Rahman to Khaleda Zia to implement reforms which would radically change the structure and composition of the public service and orientation and work habits of public servants. The response of Sheikh Hasina's government to donor reform initiatives is not clear as yet.

REFERENCES

Gant, G.E. (1979). *Development Administration: Concepts, Goals, Methods.* Wisconsin : University of Wisconsin Press.

IPA (1981). *Pre-Investment Study for a Public Administration Training and Management Improvement Project in Bangladesh*. New York: Institute of Public Administration (IPA).

Khan, M.M. (1984). "The Need for a Comprehensive National Training Policy in Bangladesh", *Management Development* 13(2) : 54-59.

Khan, M.M. (1989). "Public Administration Training Centre : A Critical Overview", in Khan, M.M. and Husain, S.A. eds. *Bangladesh Studies: Politics, Administration, Rural Development and Foreign Policy*. Dhaka: Centre for Administrative Studies, pp. 58-80.

Khan M.M. et. al. (1989). *Report of the Public Administration Efficiency Study*. (Five volumes). Washington, D.C.: Checchi and Co. Consulting Inc.

Rahman, A. et al. (1993). *Towards Better Government in Bangladesh*. Dhaka : Bangladesh Government Press.

Sobhan, R. (1982). *The Crisis of External Dependence: The Political Economy of Foreign Aid to Bangladesh*. Dhaka: University Press Limited (UPL).

Sobhan, R. and Bhattacharya, D. (1990). "Donor Perspective and Influence on Economic Policy" in Sobhan, R. ed. *From Aid Dependence to Self-Reliance: Development Options for Bangladesh*. Dhaka: UPL, pp. 177-236.

Staff Appraisal Report (1983). *Public Administration: Training, Personnel and Management Project*. Washington, D.C.: The World Bank.

Thomas, F.C. (1989). *Mobilization and Management of Public Resources in Bangladesh: A Role for UNDP'S Management Development Programme*. Dhaka: United Nations Development Programme.

UNDP (1993). *Report on Public Administration Sector Study in Bangladesh*. New York: United Nations Department of Development Support and Management Services, United Nations Development Programme.

World Bank, The (1993). *Proposed Public Administration Reform Project. Offic Memorandum.* Washington, D.C.: The World Bank.

World Bank, The (1996a). *Government that Works: Reforming the Public Sector.* Washington, D.C.: The World Bank.

CHAPTER 7

Resistance to Major Administrative Reforms in South Asian Civil Services

INTRODUCTION

Excepting Nepal, the other countries of South Asia were under British rule for a considerable period of time. Though all these countries were granted independence in late '40s, the British influence on their respective administrative systems is still considerable. This has been described as the imperial legacy which has shaped and continues to mould the administrative style and bureaucratic culture of India, Pakistan, Bangladesh and Sri Lanka. Though Nepal escaped direct colonial rule, it was not totally immune from British influence. It suited the British interest in the subcontinent to maintain the semi-colony status of Nepal under which its rulers enjoyed internal autonomy, 'in exchange for preponderant influence in foreign and trade policies' by the British (Blaikie et al., 1980: 31-32).

Overwhelming majority of the population of all these countries live in abject poverty, suffer from hunger and malnutrition, face the curse of illiteracy, forced with unemployment or underemployment and contribute to high rate of fertility. The basic needs of the majority of the population remain unfulfilled. Inequitable social system which contributes to such a deplorable situation is further reinforced by the caste system, differentiation based on religion and wealth and ethnic conflict.

The political systems of five South Asian nations do not differ much on the surface. But a close look will indicate significant differences in terms of how the systems operate in practice.

India has a parliamentary system of government. But since independence the Indian government has been dominated by members of one family. This family is known as the Nehru-Gandhi dynasty which ruled India for about thirty eight years out of fifty years of India's existence as an independent country. Also the dominance of one political party -- the Congress Party in the Indian politics has been remarkable. All the Prime Ministers of independent India were members of the Congress Party. A few of them left the party later to form their own political parties and to forge alliance with other political parties in a bid to head the government. It may be pointed out that all the Indian Prime Ministers, excepting three came from the core of one region -- the Uttar Pradesh. The present Janata Dal coalition government in the centre is weak which rules with support of the Congress Party. This was demostrated by the Congress's withdrawal of support from Deve Gowda government and its subsequent defeat in the parliamentary vote of confidence. The Congress's support enables Inder Kumar Gujral, Gowda's successor, to stay in power.

Pakistan's political history has been characterized by prolonged periods of military rule and political use of religion to suppress democratic movements. The present government is an elected one led by Mian Nawaz Sharif of Pakistan Muslim Leauge. Sharif's predecessor headed an interim government appointed by the President. Earlier the President dismissed the second elected government of Benazir Bhutto. The predecessor of Benazir Bhutto's government was that of Sharif's elected government. Sharif was earlier a close advisor and minister in the cabinet of late dictator General Mohammad Ziaul Huq who ruled Pakistan for ten years. In fact, he was a protégé of the late General. He was brought into the political arena from an obscure and non-political background by General Ziaul Huq. It is no coincidence that both Sharif and General Huq came from Punjab. It is well-known that Punjab as the region not only dominated the politics of Pakistan but also had more than its share in both the civil service and the military compared to other regions. The present President himself comes from a wealthy land-owning family of Punjab. He was also a member of the elite Civil Service of Pakistan (CSP). The Prime Minister is a rich industrialist. He built his fortune during the regime of General Huq. His brother is now the elected Chief Minister of Punjab.

Sri Lanka, after experimenting with the parliamentary system for two decades, settled for a presidential form of government for over a decade. But with the assassination of the last President, i.e. Premadasa, the loss of the then ruling party in the parliamentary elections to the opposition party and clear victory of the United National Party (UNP) in the presidential election have created an atmosphere where return to the parliamentary system is envisaged. But it should be noted that the continuous ethnic strife involving Sinhali majority and Tamil minority has considerably sapped the vitality and undermined the capability of the political system itself.

In Nepal, popular movements and mass demonstrations led to the formation of a democratic government. A Marxist political party came to power after the parliamentary elections of 1990. But in the last election of 1995 the Nepali Congress Party returned to power. The institutionalization of the democratic process has considerably reduced the power of the hereditary absolutist monarch over the affairs of the state and opened opportunities for increasing popular participation.

In all these countries, barring few exceptions, higher public servants have maintained a close relationship with the politicians and generals in power. Politicians at the helm of state affairs have found it beneficial to depend rather heavily on the 'elite' civil servants. Higher civil servants with generalist background and occupying key positions as heads of ministries and corporations have been more comfortable in working with authoritarian regimes. The authoritarian rulers, on the other hand, devoid of public support and immune from public scrutiny, have been found eager to forge alliance with these civil servants, whose patronizing attitude towards people are too well known.

MAJOR ADMINISTRATIVE REFORM EFFORTS IN SOUTH ASIAN CIVIL SERVICES

This section contains analysis of major administrative reform efforts in South Asian countries excepting Bangladesh focusing specifically on the higher civil services. From each country one or more cases have been chosen to highlight the reasons for resistance to major administrative reform proposals and consequently their non-implementation. In Pakistan where major administrative reforms succeeded have also been analysed. Inferences have also been drawn in the process of the analysis to indicate the conditions under which major administrative reforms can be implemented.

INDIA

Since independence in 1947 a number of commissions, committees and experts have been appointed to study various facets of India's administrative system and to recommend necessary changes. But none have gone deeper and examined the whole system of administration as such, and almost all have been prisoners of the existing framework and the system that underscore it (Maheshwari, 1972:15). No attempt was made to assess the utility of a highly centralized and elitist civil service, i.e. the Indian Administrative Service (IAS). The chairman of the Administrative Reforms Commission (ARC) K. Hanumanthaiya bluntly pointed out that 'during the last twenty years (1947-1966), there were only adjustments and no reforms in the administration' (*The Hindustan Times*, 28 April 1967).

The only exceptions to this trend were the reports of the ARC. The Commission was appointed in 1966 and submitted twenty reports and made a total of 581 recommendations by 1970 when it was wound up. Of these reports the one on personnel administration attracted lots of attention. We shall confine our discussion here on this particular report as this has direct bearing on the scope of this chapter.

The ARC was given a broad mandate to examine the public

administration of the country and make recommendations for reform and reorganization to ensure efficiency and maintain integrity in the public service to enable the public servants to be responsive to the people's needs. This broad mandate as well as the composition of the Commission which originally included six members of which five were politicians including the chairman, enabled it to recommend reform measures which were strikingly different from either those which preceded it or those which followed it.

The major recommendations of ARC included: (1) ending the preeminent position of IAS generalists, in the central secretariat and allowing all competent class I offices from all services, access to middle and senior management posts in the secretariat; (ii) placing people from the specialist services to man top posts in particular subject areas in the secretariat where specialist services already existed to attend to specialist subjects; and (iii) categorizing all middle level posts in non-specialist areas in the secretariat into eight broad areas of specialization and basing selection to these posts on the basis of a mid-career competitive examination from all Class I officers (Potter, 1986:169).

The recommendations of the ARC were fundamental in nature and had far reaching implications. If implemented, the recommendations would have affected the very foundation of the IAS – the elitism. The recommendations were meant to open up opportunities to all competent civil servants on the basis of proven ability irrespective of their service affiliation and thereby ending the IAS monopoly to all top posts in the central and state governments. The chairman of the ARC clearly foresaw the resistance the recommendations would generate from within the civil service. He clearly stated in his covering letter to the Prime Minister of India when submitting the Report on Personnel Administration that 'the reforms we have recommended are bound to raise resistance from those who are adversely affected. Resistance from within the service is a very difficult problem for the government to deal with' (Report on Personnel Administration, 1969: iv).

Still, none of the major recommendations of ARC were accepted by the government. The reasons for the resistance towards and consequently non-implementation of the reform proposals can be attributed to two sets of factors. First, strong and organized resistance were put up to ARC's recommendation by members of the IAS apprehending downgrading of their status if the proposals were implemented. Some senior members of the IAS at that time not only defended the elitism but developed arguments challenging the assumptions of ARC's recommendations (Chaturvedi, 1969; Dubhashi, 1969; Mohanty, 1969). The power of the IAS within the bureaucracy to control the process of administrative reform is certainly an important part of the explanation of how and why they managed to beat off the challenge of the ARC's major recommendations in the Report on Personnel Administration (Potter, 1986:171). Second, there was no strong political will to accept and implement ARC's recommendations. Political developments at the time adversely affected the prospect of the ARC. Also there was something to do with the political timing. It was the government of Lal Bahadur Shastri which announced its intention to set up an ARC in November 1965 and the plan was for the Commission to complete its work before the general elections of 1967. By the time the Commission started its work in April 1966, Indira Gandhi had taken over the Prime Ministership after the sudden death of Shastri. Also Morarji Desai, the first chairman of the ARC, was left out of the government after the split of the Congress Party in 1969. So the Commission's composition was not to the liking of the then Prime Minister Indira Gandhi. Also, 1967 general elections brought a number of non-Congress governments in the states thereby reducing the strength of the Congress government at the Centre (Potter, 1986:171). More importantly, there was broad political support from the ruling Congress Party at the Centre for the continued existence of the IAS (Potter, 1986:178).

PAKISTAN

In Pakistan, like India, many commissions, committees and experts were asked from time to time to study the administrative system and suggest improvements. Of these, five reports (Egger,

1953; Gladieux, 1955; Cornelius, 1962, 1970; Power, 1969) deserve to be discussed here as all of them thoroughly surveyed the administrative system and recommended measures to overhaul the existing system. None of the reform bodies found rationale for retaining an administrative system which had lost its usefulness and utility, and only encouraged the perpetuation of inequity and injustice in the recruitment, training, promotion, and pay among different civil services (Khan, 1980:128).

The recommendations of the five reform bodies ranged from abolition of all-Pakistan services and their replacement with a single unified civil service composed of sub-cadres of all class I officers; abolition of reservation of posts in favour of a particular cadre; abolition of the elite CSP; establishment of uniform pay structures throughout the civil service; enhanced role of specialists in the civil service; provision of lateral entry; giving comparable status to Heads of Departments and Secretaries of Ministries; raising the status of the Public Service Commission; and abolition of the Establishment Division (Kennedy, 1987: 56-64).

None of the recommendations of the five bodies were accepted. In fact between 1953 to 1972 no major changes were effectuated in the civil service system. The resistance to major administrative reforms emanated from and sustained by the members of the Civil Service of Pakistan (CSP). The CSP felt threatened by the recommendations and organized effectively to block their acceptance. The result, from the point of view of the CSPs, were remarkable. Both Egger and Gladieux reports were labeled secret and barred from public circulation for over a decade. 'As an elitist group in Pakistan bureaucracy the CSP wield(ed) tremendous power and influence . . . it was able to prevent the publication of two reports (Egger and Gladieux) which were adverse in their comments on its role and efficiency' (Sayeed, 1967: 155-56). 'He (Egger) perhaps considered too lightly that his recommendations directly threatened officials with status and power (CSP) in the administrative structure' (Gorvine, 1966 : 189). The opposition to the Pay and Services Commission, 1959-62 also known as the First Cornelius Commission was open, organized and well-orchestrated. The members of the CSP took a very active and leading role in waging a sustained campaign to block the efforts of the Commission. As an organized and privileged group within the civil service system, the CSP had everything to lose because 'such proposals deeply threatened the elite status and exclusiveness of the CSP, particularly the attack (of the Commission) on its privileged system of earmarked jobs' (Gorvine, 1966: 202).

Two members of the Commission belonging to the CSP disagreed with the majority opinion and submitted a dissenting note justifying the maintenance of the status quo. The CSP National Association expressed its solidarity in public with their two senior dissonant colleagues. One member of the CSP even took time to write to support the continuation of the preeminent position of the CSP (Husain, 1969a; 1969b). The same fate befell the Report of the Working Group on the Reorganization of the Public Service Structure prepared in light of the Fulton Committee Report, 1969, popularly known as the Power Report and the Services Reorganization Committee Report, 1970, also known as the Second Cornelius Committee Report.

Besides the CSP opposition, there was almost no political support for reform. This is understandable. After the assassination of the first Prime Minister of Pakistan in 1951, political instability became a permanent feature of the governance system. Between 1951-58 the power was in the hands of one person, the Governor-General and the President. Prime ministers and other ministers were appointed and dismissed by him at will. Also during this period no election was held to constitute a new federal legislature. The rulers preferred to continue with a legislature which was constituted in 1946 during the British time. The military was all along strongly supportive of the chief executive, a former senior civil servant. But finally, as expected, the military formally took over the reign of power in 1958. The military rule continued for thirteen years. The general who staged the coup was against any major changes in the civil service system of the country. General Ayub Khan who ruled Pakistan from 1958-1969 stated that the 'Cornelius Commission recommended radical changes involving a complete redesigning of the existing scheme and organization of public service but nothing should be done at this time which might disrupt the administrative fabric' (Khan, 1980: 106). Interestingly, it was General Ayub Khan who appointed the Commission. General Yahya Khan succeeded General Ayub Khan and continued with the same policy.

The implementation of far-reaching administrative reform proposals had to wait till the assumption of power by Zulfiqar Ali Bhutto. Bhutto's Pakistan People's Party won majority seats in the National Legislature from West Pakistan (now Pakistan) in the 1970's parliamentary elections. Bhutto, after his appointment as Prime Minister, wasted little time to overhaul the administrative system of Pakistan. Bhutto's 1973 reforms were shaped, influenced and moulded by the recommendations of Egger, Gladieux, Cornelius, 1962 and 1970 and Power, 1969.

Bhutto's administrative reforms could be termed 'revolutionary' and its salient features included:

a. Abolition of service cadres and their functional replacement by occupational groups;
b. The establishment of a Unified National Pay Scale replacing the numerous pay scales extant at the time of the reform;
c. The discontinuance of the long standing practice of reservation of certain posts in the Central Secretariat for members of the elite cadres;
d. The establishment of a programme of joint pre-service training;
e. The establishment of provisions for the introduction of lateral recruits, i.e., individuals without cadre affiliation to posts within the Central Secretariat. Provision for vertical movement between cadres was also introduced. (Kennedy, 1986: 54).

Bhutto's success in implementing major administrative reforms can be explained by looking at a number of variables. First, Bhutto had the convictions and the political will to undertake radical reforms. Second, after the 1971 war, the Pakistan military lost its credibility and was compelled to hand over power to the civilian government of Bhutto. Third, the Civil Service of Pakistan (CSP) whose consistent and dogged resistance blocked earlier reforms were defensive for the first time because they were not able to manipulate Bhutto. Bhutto was apprehensive of the military-CSP alliance which effectively ruled Pakistan since independence in 1947. Fourth, majority of the members of other civil services (excepting the CSP) wanted the dismantling of the existing system and its replacement by a reformed one. Fifth, public disenchantment with inefficiency, arrogance and corruption in the civil service reached such a stage that it could not be ignored any more. The major share of the blame went to the CSP as they were the ones who occupied key positions in the civil service and exercised authority. Civil servants, especially the CSP's, were not viewed immune from political influence. The perception was there that they needed to be reformed to be changed.

With General Ziaul Huq's seizure of state power in 1977 through a coup, the stage began of reversing the process of administrative reform initiated by the Bhutto government. The civil bureaucracy spearheaded by the members of the former CSP cadre and its successor the District Management Group started to assert itself and reemerged as a powerful group with a great deal of power and prestige (Islam, 1990:75). It is no surprise than that a large number of senior policy and administrative positions are presently occupied by members of the former CSP cadre.

SRI LANKA

From 1948 to 1956 there was no attempt on the part of the government to reform the civil service in spite of demands by opposition political parties for overhauling the inherited administrative system. A number of factors contributed to this lack of interest in major reforms (Wiswa Warnapala, 1974: 333). First, the process of 'Ceylonization' was virtually completed before independence in 1948. This Ceylonization simply meant that by that time the elite Ceylon Civil Service (CCS) was entirely manned by Ceylonese themselves. Second, there was similarity in the social background and cultural orientation of the members of CCS and the political leadership which came to power after independence in Sri Lanka. The elite civil servants and the political elite belonged to the landed gentry and were related in many cases by kinship. Third, there was conviction on the part of the political leadership that the CCS was capable of adjustment and adaptation.

The status quo within the civil service remained unchanged till 1960. After the elections of 1960 the new government declared its intention to reorganize the civil service. Keeping this objective in mind, the government appointed the Salaries and Cadre Commission popularly known as the Wilmot Perera Commission. The major recommendations of the Commission were the abolition of the elite Ceylon Civil Service (CCS) and constitution of a Unified Administrative Service. The Commission in its report submitted in 1961 spelled out the nature of the unified service. The members of the service would be chosen on the basis of a uniform method of recruitment providing equal opportunities to all civil servants for entry into the higher echelons of the civil service, the need for unification in the civil service was recognized as early as 1953 by the Poulier Commission.

Though the government accepted the recommendations of the Wilmot Perera Commission, it did not implement the body's recommendations in full. As a result of the partial implementation of the recommendations, the Ceylon Administrative Service (CAS) was formed in place of Sri Lanka Administrative Service (SLAS). All the administrative officers above the executive level, belonging to CAS and other departmental cadres were absorbed into the CAS. The manner in which various categories of civil servants were absorbed in the CAS seemed to be discriminatory. Under the rule of absorption . . . officers belonging to the (erstwhile) CAS were absorbed into Classes IV to I, but the bulk of the officers from the Administrative Grades and Services were absorbed into one of the two grades in Class V, the lowest class. Only a few (non-CAS officers) were absorbed into higher classes. This resulted in anomalous situation such as District Land Officers with twenty years' service being placed below CAS cadets with one year's service' (Navaratne, 1980:70).

The reform efforts have not succeeded in bringing about major changes within the Sri Lankan public service system. The members of the SLAS, remnant of the colonial CCS, continue to enjoy both prestige and status far disproportionate to their actual size. There is little doubt that members of SLAS have significant influence on the outcome of any major reform effort within the public service system.

Although no major reforms have been effectuated in the civil service system, increasing politicization of the bureaucracy has continued unabated. Personal loyalty to the minister and party in power has now become the most important virtue of a civil servant in place of dedication and devotion to the state (Wijeweera, 1989:292). There has not been political will to build a civil service based on meritocracy and security of service. Also the elite civil servants have not been eager to give up power which they have enjoyed for so many years.

NEPAL

Attempts at modernizing and reforming Nepalese administrative system started with the end of Rana Administration in 1951. During the Rana Rule the administration was intended to serve the Prime Minister who always came from the Rana family. The civil servants collected land revenues and customs duties and maintained law and order. They were poorly paid and had no tenure.

Beginning from 1952 to 1976 a number of foreign experts and four commissions examined various facets pertaining to the Nepalese civil service and made a number of major recommendations. The reform efforts ranged from formulation of appropriate rules and regulations, preparation of manuals, the setting up of an O & M office and establishment of a training programme in public administration (Panday, 1989:323).

Of all the reform initiatives the formation of the Administrative Reform Planning Commissions (ARPC) in 1956 was the landmark development in the history of public administration reform in Nepal for a number of reasons. First, the ARPC was the first indigenous Commissions with a broad scope of work to survey and analyze all aspects of the civil service system in Nepal. Second, the Commission was headed by the then Nepalese Prime Minister Tanka Prasad Acharya who commanded public respect for his integrity. Third, ARPC's modus operandi was not writing and submitting reports for later consideration, but discussion, decisions and implementation right through (Panday, 1989: 324).

The significant products of the ARPC which were effectuated included: organizing the civil service into eight cadres; organization of an O&M office; activating the Public Service Commission; establishment of the Institute of Public Administration and the setting up of Nepal Rastrya (State) Bank (Poudyal, 1984:92).

But the major reform measures of ARPC initiated and implemented under the guidance of the then Prime Minister could not run its full course. Acharya was dismissed by King Mahendra after in office for only eighteen months. This was clearly a setback for the continuation of the process of administrative reform. Other efforts to reform the civil service have not fared well. In 1959, Prime Minister B. P. Koirala attempted to implement measures that would have brought dynamism in the civil service. His measures included revoking of obstructing acts, rules, regulations, and structures; activating the Public Service Commission; increasing salaries of civil servants; prohibiting civil servants from seeking support from the Royal Palace for their protection and promotion; and fixing expenditures of Royal Palace (Poudyal, 1989:121-125). Koirala suffered the same fate as that of Acharya.

The resistance to major administrative reforms in Nepal has been explained rather cogently (Panday, 1989:323-35). First, Nepal's governing coalition has not been in favour of a strong career civil service which the reforms intended as the latter might challenge the former in course of time for share of state power. Second, administrative reforms were intended to seek external legitimacy for the regime and donor support. Consequently, there have been more enthusiasm in creating new administrative structures in such a manner as to produce desired results, i.e., better public service. The recommendations of the Jha Commission, 1965 and the Thapa Commission, 1975 for the reduction of number of ministries were not implemented even after the government's acceptance of the recommendations. Instead, the number of ministries increased in both instances. The Public Service Commission is routinely ignored in matters pertaining to public personnel management.

CONCLUSION

Several conclusions emerge from the foregoing analysis of the experiences of initiating and implementing major administrative reform proposals in South Asian civil services. First, lack of political will and commitment on the part of political leadership has been the key determinant in the failure of major administrative reform efforts. Successive political leaderships in all these countries except for the Bhutto government in Pakistan from 1972-77 found it expedient to publicly profess the need for radical overhaul the public service systems. Their public commitment was limited to setting up of reform bodies and appointment of other bodies mostly composed of senior civil servants to scrutinize the recommendations of various reform commissions and committees. Second, the civil servants belonging to elite cadres like the IAS in India, the CSP in Pakistan and the CSS in Sri Lanka have been the vanguard of resistance to any attempts to change the status quo. They have usually been successful because of the political leadership's undue dependence on them. Third, there has not been any organized reform movement by any major segment of the society in the South Asian countries to offset bureaucratic resistance and political apathy towards major administrative reforms.

REFERENCES

Blaikie, P. et al. (1980). *Nepal in Crisis: Growth and Stagnation at the Periphery*. Delhi: Oxford University Press.

Chaturvedi, M.K. (1969). "Personnel Administration: The Need for Realism", *Indian Journal of Public Administration* (IJPA) 15:32-73.

Egger, R. (1953). *The Improvement of Public Administration in Pakistan: A Report with Recommendations*. (Mimeo.) Karachi.

Gladieux, B. (1955). *Reorientation of Pakistan Government for National Development*. (Photostat) Karachi.

Dubhashi, P.R. (1969). "ARC's Report on Personnel Administration: Faulty Superstructure on False Premises", *IJPA*, 15:623-34.

Gorvine, A. (1966). "Administrative Reform: Function of Economic and Political Change", in Birkhead, G.S. ed. *Administrative Problems in Pakistan*. Syracuse: Syracuse University Press, pp. 185-211.

Government of Pakistan (GOP) (1969). *Report of the Pay and Services Commission, 1959-1962*. Karachi: Cabinet Division, MPCPP.

GOP (1969). *Report of the Working Group on the Reorganization of the Public Service Structure (in the light of the Fulton Report)*. Karachi : MPCPP.

Husain, I. (1969a). "An Analysis of the Assumptions Made in the Cornelius Report", *NIPA Journal*, 10:90-100.

Husain, I. (1969b). "Conceptual Analysis of Civil Service Reform in Pakistan", *Administrative Science Review*, 3:64-76.

India (1969). *Report on Personnel Administration*. New Delhi: Administrative Reforms Commission.

Islam, N. (1990). "Pakistan", in Subramaniam, V. ed. *Public Administration in the Third World*. New York: Greenwood Press, pp. 68-101.

Kennedy, C.H. (1987). *Bureaucracy in Pakistan*. Karachi: Oxford University Press.

Khan, M.M. (1980). *Bureaucratic Self Preservation: Failure of Major Administrative Reform Efforts in the Civil Service of Pakistan*. Dhaka: University of Dhaka.

Maheshwari, S. (1972). "Administrative Reforms: Historical Prospects", in Maheshwari, S. *The Administrative Reform Commission*. Agra:L.N. Agarwal.

Mohanty, N. (1969). "ACR on Personnel Administration: Study in Bias", *IJPA*, 15:635-55.

Navaratne, V.T. (1980). "The Evolution of Administrative Service in Sri Lanka". In: Navaratne, V.T. ed. *Current Issues in Public Personnel Management in Sri Lanka*. Colombo: Sri Lanka Institute of Development Administration, pp.65-82.

Panday, D.R.(1989). "Administrative Development in a Semi-dependence: The Experience of Nepal", *PA&D*, 9:315-329.

Potter, D.C. (1989). *India's Political Administrators, 1919-1983*. Oxford: Clarendon Press.

Poudyal, M.P. (1984). *Public Administration and Nation Building in Nepal*. Delhi:National Book Organization.

Poudyal, M.P. (1989). *Administrative Reforms in Nepal*. Delhi: National

Book Organization.

Wiswa Warnapala, W.A. (1974). *Civil Service Administration in Ceylon: A Study in Bureaucratic Adaptation.* Colombo: Department of Cultural Affairs.

Wijeweera, B.S. (1989). "Policy Developments and Administrative Changes in Sri Lanka, 1948-1987", *PA&D*, 9:287-300.

CHAPTER 8

Coping with Twenty-first Century: Experiences of Commonwealth Countries & Prescriptions for Bangladesh

INTRODUCTION

Major administrative reform initiatives have not been successful so far in Bangladesh. The public service the way it is designed and operates is not suitable to meet the demands of the citizens. It is clear that in view of the changed social, political and economic scenario there is an urgency to radically reform the public service. Tinkering and minor adjustments will not be enough. The challenges of the twenty-first century which lie ahead must be faced boldly with a reformed, revitalized and dynamic public service. The democratic system which is in operation for last six years is slowly being institutionalized in the context of intolerance, bickering and violence. The concept of non-partisan caretaker government, for the interim period to hold parliamentary elections, has been accepted by all political parties. In the economic arena there is continuing emphasis to encourage increasing participation of the private sector in the national life. The social scene provides a picture of deterioration of moral values buttressed by the desire to move up in the social ladder using whatever means are available at one's disposal.

The brief description above of the changed socio-politico and economic scene makes one thing crystal clear. The public service must change and corresponding changes must also result in work ethics and attitudes of public servants. Otherwise, Bangladesh will not be able to survive let alone prosper in the highly competitive world market.

This concluding chapter includes discussion as to how other Commonwealth countries have reformed their public services to face the challenges of the twenty-first century; and recommendations as to how the public service in Bangladesh can also be revamped, revitalized and reformed in order to confidently tackle the ever-changing and complex world of today and tomorrow. In making the recommendations the experiences of other Commonwealth countries along with the fundamental deficiencies afflicting the public service in Bangladesh have been kept in mind. It is understood also that significant differences exist between Bangladesh and some Commonwealth countries in terms of social, political, economic and cultural variables. It is also believed that in spite of the differences, experiences of other Commonwealth countries can be useful for policy makers and policy planners in initiating and implementing major administrative reforms.

EXPERIENCES OF COMMONWEALTH COUNTRIES

Many commonwealth countries, irrespective of population size, resource-base and geographical location, have had to face the difficult task of initiating, managing and implementing reforms in the public sector. They adopted similar strategies by re-defining the relationship between policy-making and administration; introducing greater accountability, task-definition, performance measurement and delegation of the control of resources; the need for closer collaboration with organizational review; and the importance of the quality of service (Commonwealth Secretariat, 1995:v). Problems confronting the public service could not be solved without looking at them from a radically different perspective. It is not enough to find solutions banking on such variables as political will, relevant ideas and managerial initiatives. Increasingly in recent years the focus has been on the role of the state. Many consider that without agreement on a changed role of the state nothing much can be achieved. The domain of the state must be considerably reduced. Consequently, serious thinking need to be given to refocusing and narrowing the role and responsibilities of governmental institutions. What is visualized is a new role and style of government buttressed by a new managerial approach.

The experiences of Commonwealth countries indicate that for sustaining public service reform programmes a number of factors and/or variables should be present. These are considered as components of a framework within which changes take place.

Political Commitment

High-level political support given by politicians in power and senior civil servants is a decisive factor in successful implementation of reforms in the public service. In UK, Canada, New Zealand, Jamaica, Malaysia and Singapore successful reforms received support and encouragement from heads of governments as well as chief executives of organizations suggest that sustainable commitment has three elements at both political and managerial levels. These levels are:

> First, commitment to change involves a willingness to indicate a clear preference for the future; to say what an improved public service would look like and what it is in the past that must be left behind. Second, it also entails a willingness to take responsibility for, to own and to accept praise and blame, for the process that will lead to that future. Finally, commitment requires a preparedness to describe and repeat, as often as possible both that preference for the future and the process for getting there (Commonwealth Secretariat, 1995:15).

The above detailing of levels clearly operationalizes political commitment vis-a-vis major administrative reforms. Vision for future on the part of political and managerial leaders is the crucial ingredient in political commitment.

A Credible Pace for Reform

Successful reform programmes, irrespective of their nature and coverage, must have credibility. This credibility should not be confined to any particular group. The experiences of New Zealand and Mauritius indicate that though there were differences among the two in terms of the pace of reform both worked within given constraints and promised what they could realistically offer (Commonwealth Secretariat, 1995:15-16). Credibility of a reform programme to all -- politicians, people and civil servants -- determines to a large extent its eventual success.

A Focal Point for Change

Experiences of two African countries, i.e. Uganda and Zambia confirm the hypothesis that implementation of comprehensive reform programmes depend on a strategically placed central unit competent to monitor progress and if required to guide progress (Commonwealth Secretariat, 1995:16).

Ownership Across the Public Service

The management of change in the public service makes it almost imperative that public servants at different levels in the hierarchy to be involved in the process and share the vision and want change (Commonwealth Secretariat, 1995:7). The importance of ownership of major reforms by all in the public service is clearly noticed in countries like New Zealand and Trinidad and Tobago.

Balancing Consumer Expectations

Public service improvements in many Commonwealth countries have resulted due to high level of expectations of citizens as consumers of services and goods. But to match citizen demands managerial expectations also must increase. The experiences of Singapore, Namibia and the UK are pertinent in this context. Singapore civil service has encouraged raising of public expectations of service standards while performance evaluation and accountability mechanisms are being strengthened in Namibian civil service so that each and every citizen knows what kind of services can be expected (Commonwealth Secretariat, 1995:17-18). In the UK the citizen's charter initiative is an attempt to create awareness among citizens as to the standards to be expected from public services (Commonwealth Secretariat, 1995:18).

FEELING THE CONSEQUENCES OF SERVICES

Some Commonwealth countries have been successful in institutionalizing systems of feedback in the public services to ensure that improvements or deterioration are detected and so that appropriate actions can be taken. Performance management systems are utilized to link achievements against organizational goals as well as budget allocations are being increased to high-performing organizations at the expense of those whose performance have not been satisfactory (Commonwealth Secretariat, 1995:18). In Zambia performance targets are now very much part of the public service while in the UK school funding is conditioned by the popularity of the schools with parents.

BUILDING INSTITUTIONAL SUPPORT OUTSIDE

Effective public service depends on interconnected network of civil society organizations and interest groups, whose specific concerns are harnessed to support public service performance as many managerial options proposed for inclusion within public service reform programmes rest on the capacity of external civil, professional and political institutions (Commonwealth Secretariat, 1995: 18-19). In Ghana, a nation-wide programme, the National Institutional Renewal Programme is prepared in such a way so that the public sector institutions are strengthened and public service improvement becomes a constituent of the larger programme.

OPEN-ENDED CONTINUOUS CHANGE

It is now accepted that reforms are part of the public service as pace of change is to increase in future to cope with challenges. The reforms instituted in Malta noted that there were specific aspects of the service that must be improved urgently and at the sametime they recognized that there was a long-term, open-ended process of reform ahead (Commonwealth Secretariat, 1995:19).

Beside the above-mentioned eight components of a framework for change, seven practical strategies have been identified within reform programmes undertaken in Commonwealth countries. These are: improving policy development and coordination, restructuring the organization, reorienting the organizational culture, managing human resources, commercializing and developing partnerships, improving financial planning and control systems and harnessing information technology (Commonwealth Secretariat, 1995:20).

PRESCRIPTIONS FOR CHANGE IN BANGLADESH

The public service in Bangladesh is in the throes of crisis. It is characterized by a rigid structure, low productivity, overarching reach, lack of delegation of authority, recruitment not totally based on merit, inappropriate training and not need-based, promotion not linked with performance, irrational transfer, constant inter-cadre feud and pay not linked to performance and productivity. The result of the crisis is evident in poor quality of service, lack of service orientation among civil servants, endemic corruption, lack of accountability and transparency, inefficiency, ineffectiveness and rising cost for maintaining the public sector.

The World Bank in a recent report points out succinctly what ails the public sector in Bangladesh. Some of reasons for such a pathetic condition are:

> A state apparatus that extends well beyond the core functions of the state. Unpredictable and sometimes covert decision making and weak accountability that make government actions nontransparent. A complex, oversized and nearly unmanageable bureaucracy and institutional opparatus. Badly motivated and underpaid public employees at the senior and mid-management levels (World Bank, 1996a:57).

The discussion which follows concentrates on what should be done to reform the public service and how this can be accomplished. The discussion proceeds in light of the experiences of the Commonwealth countries, global trends in the area of public service reform as well as limitations of the government of Bangladesh.

RIGHTSIZING THE GOVERNMENT

It is now apparent that government involvement and intervention in each and every aspect of a citizen's life is neither possible nor feasible. But this has been the case in Bangladesh. The number of ministries, departments and civil servants,. have doubled since independence. The reasons behind such an increase has been threefold (World Bank, 1996a:17). To meet emerging needs and concerns in such areas as environment and women, new governmental institutions were set up. Increasing involvement of the state in commercial activities also demanded new organizations in the public sector. Also ministries and divisions were created to accommodate political elements and faction leaders and consequently more avenues opened in the process for politicians to give jobs to their key supporters. Therefore it is no wonder that the number of ministries in Bangladesh stands at 35 which is considerably large compared to other countries such as Malayasia (24), South Korea (25), Thailand (14), Japan (14) and U.K. (16) (World Bank, 1996a:17). Not only ministries but there have been corresponding increase in the number of personnel in the public sector organizations in Bangladesh. The public sector employs a million people in 35 ministries, 50 divisions, 221 departments, 139 directorates and autonomous bodies and 153 state enterprises (World Bank, 1996b:57).

In view of the present situation, a number of actions need to be taken to rightsize the government. The premises on which actions are recommended include: (i) government is not in the business of providing employment to its citizens on a regular and continuous basis without taking into consideration the need and costs involved; and (ii) public service jobs are not meant to be used to dole out political favours.

First, all posts that remain vacant in the public sector for a considerable period of time, i.e. one to two years should be abolished. Second, redundancies in the government should be tackled by significantly reducing the number of ministries, divisions, departments, directorates and subordinate offices in accordance with the actual needs. Third, administrative heads of all government agencies should be instructed by a designated agency, a unit within the Prime Minister's Secretariat, to review functions, work load and performance of their organizations twice a year and send specific proposals to the latter to reduce a percentage of their sanctioned posts and manpower. Fourth, voluntary retirement of civil servants, especially those at the lower rung of the hierarchy, should be encouraged. At the sametime, the practice to reappoint senior civil servants on contract basis after they reach compulsory retirement age should be discontinued. Fifth, contracting out of selected functions and services of public sector agencies to private sector organizations should begin immediately.

Open Structure

The way public service structure is organized in Bangladesh encourages inter-service tensions between cadres, between cadres and non-cadres and non-cadres and between class 1 officers and class II, III, IV officers and staff (UNDP, 1993:63).

The measure recommended here is the adoption of the open structure for the public service in Bangladesh. To introduce open structure, two actions should be taken simultaneously. First, different classes and cadres within the public service should be abolished. Second, a single classless Unified Grading Structure (UGS) should be introduced. The proposed UGS would contain grades with appropriate number of pay scales matching different levels of skills and responsibility. Correct grading for each post should be determined by job analysis. The UGS can be operationalized by improved job descriptions to clarify both agencies expectations of public servants and the linkages between tasks, standards, skills and minimum qualifications.

Enhancing Accountability

A major problem in Bangladesh's public sector is not only lack of accountability but also the nature of accountability itself as the chain of accountability stretching from the parliament to class IV employees is weak and fuzzy; many of the links have been severed, resulting in the inability to enforce financial contracts, stop theft in public enterprises or hold officials accountable for improper or delayed judgment (World Bank, 1996a: viii). Traditional internal mechanisms like hierarchy and supervision have mostly failed.

A number of actions should be taken to institutionalize political control over civil service and to substantially improve performance within governmental agencies. First, parliamentary accountability lies at the heart of good governance especially in a democratic system of government. A number of steps need to be taken to strengthen parliamentary accountability. One of the first measures in this direction would be the establishment of a bi-partisan parliamentary task force to strengthen the standing committees, instituting the practice of questioning ministers and providing members of parliament with adequate office and research facilities and establishing an office of ombudsman (World Bank, 1996a: viii). Also a parliamentary secretariat should be established outside the sphere of the civil service and be manned by competent personnel recruited separately and controlled by the speaker of the parliament. Second, to ensure financial accountability the office of the Comptroller and Auditor General (CAG) must be reorganized and strengthened by enhancing the capacity of the CAG, allowing CAG direct contacting of auditing firms, initiating programmes to undertake comprehensive audits and separating the audit from accounting function (World Bank 1996a: ix). Third, the standards of performance of the ministries/divisions and their affiliated agencies should be made known to the citizens (Rahman et al., 1993: 52). Fourth, complaint procedures should be in place in government agencies for wider use of citizens. A register should be maintained containing information about the timing and nature of complaint. Fifth, monitoring procedures need to be tightened so that the concerned senior civil servant knows the extent of compliance by subordinates to relevant orders and directives as well as services provided to the citizens. Fifth, units be established in each ministry and division to develop and apply performance criteria and measures and to develop internal performance audit capability (UNDP, 1993:106).

Ensuring Transparency

Public sector decision making is non-transparent. Bureaucrats value secrecy and not willing to inform public how decisions are taken. Openness and transparency are alien concepts in the public bureaucracy in Bangladesh. A number of actions are recommended to ensure transparency and thereby considerably empower citizens (World Bank, 1996a: xii). First, the Official Secrets Act of 1923 and Government Service Conduct Rules of 1979 need to be suitability modified. Second, a task force on public sector transparency should be established with membership from different professional and occupational groups to suggest measures to enhance transparency. Third, necessary steps need to be taken to make all contract evaluations reports public thereby enabling all bidders to see how evaluations were made. Still other steps can be taken to ensure transparency. Fourth, earning and tax payments of elected as well as appointed officials can be published on a yearly basis. Fifth, interested citizens must be allowed access to relevant files and documents. Such inspection of files and documents will enable affected citizens to understand the process and dynamics of decisions taken within the context of existing rules and regulations. This can help citizens to accept decisions of public servants that have gone against them, i.e. fixation of rate of municipal and income taxes. Sixth, number of files marked secret and top secret should be drastically reduced to encourage more frequent inspection of more files by citizens and facilitate free-flow of information. Seventh, civil servants long accustomed to transact public business under the veil of secrecy, should be appropriately trained and indoctrinated to bring about necessary changes in their attitudes and work habits.

ERADICATING CORRUPTION

It is well known fact that corruption thrives in Bangladesh especially in the public service. Corruption in the public sector in Bangladesh is attributed to monopoly, weak accountability mechanisms and poor pay (World Bank, 1996a: xii). A number of measures have been suggested to eradicate corruption from the public service in Bangladesh (World Bank, 1996a: xii and Rahman et al., 1993:97). First, a high-powered task force be established consisting of public officials, parliamentarians and leading public citizens to review all relevant issues pertaining to corruption and to suggest a comprehensive eradication programme. Second, an autonomous standing committee be formed with judges, senior officials and leading citizens to oversee the activities of the Bureau of Anti-Corruption (BAC) as well as authorize investigation of senior officials in ministries, corporations and other agencies by a statutory appointed and protected public prosecutor. Third, full use need to be made of BAC's own investigators as prosecutors when necessary. Also other measures can be taken to combat corruption. Fourth, salary and benefits of public servants must be at par with their counterparts in the private sector. Paying a decent salary will significantly reduce the tendency to indulge in corruption. Fifth, there should be provision for severe punishment if public servants are found to be involved in corruption including long stay in jails and confiscation of property. This measure, if effectively applied, will considerably deter public servants involvement in corrupt activities. Sixth, accountability mechanisms and measures along with increasing transparency in public dealing as suggested earlier will facilitate the ushering in of an honest and clean public service.

DELEGATION OF AUTHORITY

Centralized control and top-down direction have contributed to stifling of initiatives at different levels in the hierarchy, close supervision, slow decision making and blind adherence to rules and regulations.

To facilitate delegation of authority in the public service in Bangladesh a number of actions should be taken. First, increasing delegation of administrative and financial powers to different successive layers within ministries and divisions as well as to departments, directorates, subordinate offices, corporations, autonomous and semi-autonomous bodies be given. Second, to ensure delegation of authority to subordinate units in the government, appropriate changes need to be made in documents like the Rules of Business and the Secretariat Instructions which contain rules and regulations that govern relationships between political rulers and public servants as well as among public servants serving at different levels in the bureaucratic hierarchy. Third, delegation of authority is invariably linked with such variables as intra-and inter-ministerial coordination, multiplicity of decision making layers, channels and processes of communication and allocated time for disposal of business. So timely and meaningful changes in these variables need to be brought about to facilitate increasing delegation of administrative and financial authority down the hierarchy and units. Multiplicity of layers, among others, create redundancies and slows down decision making. Fourth, actions should be initiated to decentralize in a progressive manner policy decisions pertaining to personnel to ministries, divisions, departments, directorates, corporations, autonomous and semi-autonomous bodies.

MERIT-BASED SELECTION

The recruitment and selection (R&S) process in the public service in Bangladesh is characterized by a lack of clear-cut and well-defined recruitment policy; provision of reservation of posts ; lack of objectivity and archaic form and contents of tests and relegation of the status of the Bangladesh Public Service Commission (BPSC) vis-a-vis the Ministry of Establishment (MOE). All these have created anomalies, contradictions, confusions and deficiencies in the R&S process.

Merit-based selection in the public service can be ensured if the following actions are taken. First, each and every selection should be based on merit. Merit in this context means that entrance into the public service at different levels should be based on performance in open competitive examinations and/or demonstrated professional qualifications, expertise and experience. Second, measures should be taken to progressively limit the scope of quota (reservation) system with the objective of its eventual withdrawal within a specified time period. Third, in view of the gradual deterioration in the quality of the civil servants and educational system of the country, introduction of a two-tier recruitment system premised on accelerated upward mobility for bright, talented and outstanding civil servants is a must. Specially-designed tests would be devised and administered by the BPSC to those public servants who had completed five years of services to spot the 'high flyers'. The successful ones, after completion of appropriate training at the Bangladesh Public Administration Training Centre (BPATC), would be given challenging assignments for a period of two to three years. After the completion of that period the performance of these civil servants would be evaluated by a team consisting of BPSC members and secretaries of relevant ministries. Only those civil servants whose assessments had been highly satisfactory would be placed on a 'fast track' with the provision of review of their performance every five years to determine their career progression. Fourth, in view of the yawning gap between task performance and quality of personnel especially at the mid- and top levels, lateral entry of professionally-qualified individuals from relevant disciplines need to be institutionalized. Their qualifications, experience and expertise would be assessed by a high-powered team consisting of the chairman, BPSC, top functionaries of recognized professional bodies and secretaries of relevant ministries. Fifth, the capability of the BPSC in terms of personnel, equipment and activities need to be considerably enhanced. Politicization in terms of appointing ruling party's supporters to the posts of chairman and members of the BPSC must be stopped. Sixth, clear delimitation of the role of the BPSC vis-a-vis the MOE is urgently needed to enable the former autonomy in terms of policy decisions and day-to-day functioning. Seventh, a comprehensive R&S policy needs to be formulated taking into consideration the present reality and the future challenges confronting the public service. The cornerstone of such a policy should be merit.

NEED-BASED TRAINING

Public sector training has been characterized by a lack of clear, bold and innovative training policy; poor quality of training and dearth of well-trained and professional corps of trainers; training curriculum mostly based on foreign models and rarely updated; teaching methods mostly classroom-based and lack relevant practical exposure; proliferation of training institutions; training not linked to career development; absence of appropriate evaluation of training programmes; and tendency to appoint career civil servants to directorial posts in premier training institutions.

The need of the hour is to impart such training to public servants in Bangladesh that is useful and relevant. Hence the emphasis is on need-based training. For that to happen a number of policy decisions need to be adopted. First, a national training policy (NTP), with input from professionals and public servants of all types, need to be formulated to meet the challenges that lie ahead. The proposed training policy should contain specific guidelines, among other things, as how to link training with career planning. Second, the National Training Council's (NTC) role should be specified and its membership should include civil servants as well as specialists from such disciplines as management and public administration. The NTC is to act as an apex body where deliberations should include how to operationalize and implement the guidelines to be contained in the proposed NTP keeping in view government's policy preferences and review of achievements and problems in the area of public sector training. Third, training should be clearly linked to a public servant's career planning and progression. Training should become a necessary tool for a public servant to do his job more efficiently. There must be an appropriate fit between the task at hand as well as future assignments and types of training one receives or will receive at a later date. Fourth, professional trainers should have adequate opportunity for career movement, entitled to attractive pay and other allowances and scope for further professional development to attract and retain qualified trainers. Fifth, there should be regular evaluation of various training programmes to assess their utility in terms of enhanced capacity and increased efficiency of trainees in their jobs. Sixth, mechanisms need to be devised to facilitate more contact and cooperation of the public sector training institutions with those in the private sector. This will enable both parties to draw upon each other's experience as well as sharing of resources and personnel for mutual benefit.

Promotion Linked to Performance

There is widespread dissatisfaction among civil servants regarding the promotion system. Promotion is usually not perceived as a reward for a job well done. The distrust mainly centres on how the evaluation is made when a case for promotion is considered.

Linking promotion with performance of civil servants is needed. For that to happen a number of actions must be taken. First, there should be a clear and unambiguous understanding at the highest political level that merit should be the sole criterion for promotion of civil servants. Second, mechanisms must be designed and in place to correctly evaluate performance. The present mechanisms like Annual Confidential Reports (ACRs) and interviews have been found to be deficient in objectively assessing the performance of civil servants. Third, qualified professionals be involved in designing appropriate evaluation mechanisms to be used in future promotion exercises. Fourth, there needs to be a sea-change in the attitudes of civil servants towards promotion. They should realize that promotion is earned through one's hard work, diligence and productivity and not merely as a result of incumbency.

The discussions above concentrated on what specific measures should be taken to bring about reforms in the public service in Bangladesh. But at the sametime it is to be understood and appreciated that the most difficult stage in any reform process is the implementation stage. The discussions that follow will emphasize on the presence of some key variables and institutional mechanisms as preconditions for successful implementation and institutionalization of major administrative reform measures. It is believed that the presence of such critical variables and mechanisms will create a conducive environment for ushering in and sustenance of major reforms in the public service in Bangladesh.

POLITICAL WILL

The main driving force behind successful implementation of major administrative reform measures has been and continues to be political will on the part of politicians in power. This significant variable has been conspicuous by its absence in Bangladesh vis-a-vis major reform implementation. The experience in Bangladesh clearly suggests that politicians have not been serious in overhauling the inherited bureaucratic system. They talked about reform but did almost nothing about it.

Political commitment is the prerequisite if significant and meaningful administrative reform measures are to be implemented. It is now time for the Awami Leauge government to demonstrate through its actions and deeds that it is hundred percent in favour of a reformed public service which is in tune with changed international and domestic demands and priorities. Political guidance and direction are needed to chart a course of action which would be different from those in the past. The political leaders must be able and willing to present a vision for the future of the country and to show where and how the public service would fit into it. So courage, conviction, bold and innovative actions are needed to make a clear break with past failures and make a new beginning. But a new beginning is not always possible without costs and risks. Political leadership must be willing to take risks and own both failures and successes and not try to shift the blame on the faceless public servants. Policies and priorities of the government should be focused towards the future and not wasting time to minutely dissecting the failures of the past. The role of the Prime Minister would be to unite and lead the nation to bring about the much-needed reforms indicated earlier. Here her leadership qualities will face severe test. She can find solace from the fact that other heads of governments in the Commonwealth countries had to go through the same process and many came out successful. Public service reform should be at the top of her policy agenda. She must demonstrate her government's commitment to major administrative reforms by undertaking radical and innovative measures to bring about thorough yet meaningful changes in the public service in Bangladesh.

Bureaucratic Reorientation

It is well-established that resistance from within resulted in the non-implementation of major administrative reform measures suggested by various government-appointed commissions and committees and donors. Bureaucratic culture in Bangladesh was developed and shaped by colonial heritage of British and Pakistani rule. Maintenance of the status quo and resistance to change have become the hallmarks of bureaucratic culture.

Unless there is significant change in the beliefs, values and attitudes of the members of the public service there is little prospect that meaningful changes would result. Indoctrination must begin at the top ladder of the public service because from this level leadership is provided to obstruct, misdirect and nullify reform proposals that seek to do away with the vested interest. Public servants must be convinced that it is in their interest to accept and welcome change. Otherwise, the very foundation on which the public service stands will face severe scrutiny and eventually will be forced to live with a public service that is bound to be much smaller in size and significantly short on credibility. Public servants must own reforms and accept changes.

Civil Society

It is now certain that a government alone may not be able to bring about radical changes in an institutional bureaucracy. Other forces in the society must be organized to lend their support for a reformed public service. So effective involvement of non-governmental organizations (NGOs), private development organizations (PVDOs), professional associations, interest groups and political parties is needed as effective components of the civil society in Bangladesh to bring about changes in the age-old bureaucratic system. This will give a significant boost to changes needed in the public service. But for this to happen the civil society in Bangladesh should accord top priority to a reformed bureaucracy in its agenda and start a time-bound movement to realize its goal. It needs to be mentioned that it would not be difficult specially for NOGs, given their track record in the field of poverty eradication, to mount and sustain systematic and meaningful campaign for a reformed public service that would be accountable, transparent and service-oriented.

Role of Donors

All international donors have been critical of the role of public service in Bangladesh. The displeasure of the donor community about the efficiency and performance of public servants is an open secret. A number of donors sponsored studies of the public service system. All the studies pointed out deficiencies of the public service system or parts of it and recommended measures for overcoming such ills. But the governments of Ershad and Khaleda Zia did nothing more than constituting committees manned by top civil servants to review donor-sponsored study reports. Nothing came out of such exercises excepting giving much needed time to both the governments to stall donor pressure for reform.

Past experiences indicate that international donors must take a number of interrelated actions. First, the donors should meet and decide on a joint strategy as how to effectively persuade as well as to pressurize the government to move towards major changes and reforms in the public service. Second, implementation of major administrative reforms should be tied to aid in non-developmental projects. Third, international donors should be involved in one capacity or another in the implementation of reforms suggested by bodies funded by them. International donors also could play a catalytic role in promoting reform in the public service by:

providing institution building support;
establishing in their own programmes accountability measures and performance standards which should be widely disseminated;
ensuring user participation, undertaking customer surveys, and including responsive measures in their programmes and in implementation agencies supported by them, enhancing flow of information of their operation, particularly implementation performance, to the civil society;
incorporating "lessons of success" in their programmes and critically scrutinizing and questioning prevalent way of doing business before finalizing programme/project design;
proactively identifying and encouraging agents of change, supporting local think tanks and policy research in ministries to internalize this debate and keep it alive; and
supporting local media in its role as watchdog and as a forum for debate on imperatives for and modalities of reform (World Bank 1996a: xxii).

In other words, important and proactive role for international donors in reform implementation is recommended in view of the dependence of Bangladesh on external assistance. The leverage that international donors have over the Bangladesh government need to be used judiciously but at the sametime firmly with the intention to usher in far-reaching changes in the public service.

Reform Implementation Body

Most major reforms fail at the implementation level. Bangladesh provides a case to substantiate the thesis that high attrition rate of major reforms at the implementation stage is a reality. The major reason is the way the implementation committees are constituted. These committees are manned exclusively by senior civil servants. Most of these civil servants by virtue of their orientation and work habits are reactive, conservative and pro-establishment. They are afraid of change and prone to resist any move which would disrupt the status quo. It is no wonder that most of the reform measures had a premature death during deliberations in these committees. Reform measures were attacked as impractical, costly and useless. Reforms had no support in the bureaucratic hierarchy.

To overcome the problems of reform implementation, a high-powered permanent reform implementation body to be known as Reform Implementation Commission (RIC) should be set up immediately. The RIC is to be headed by the Prime Minister and is to be located in her secretariat. The Establishment Minister is to act as her deputy. In the absence of the Prime Minister he would preside over the meetings of RIC and oversee its day-to-day activities. He would be accountable to the Prime Minister. The Commission's membership would include relevant professionals from outside the government and generalist, technical and functional civil servants. A balance had to be maintained between professionals and public servants so that the latter cannot dominate the former using their numerical numbers and positions in the bureaucratic hierarchy. The main functions of RIC would be to spearhead change, to design reforms, to put them to work and to monitor their implementation (The World Bank, 1996b:59). The Commission would be also expected to provide the analytical underpinnings for reform, adopt a total quality management approach, formulate specific proposals and strategies and raise awareness of the need for change (The World Bank, 1996b:59).

An overarching role for RIC is visualized. Its scope of operation would be wide. It would be run like a professional organization with knowledgeable, committed and proactive individuals. All personnel would have to perform their responsibilities with a missionary zeal. In other words, it would not be allowed to degenerate into a typical bureaucrat-dominated body constituted to resist change and pass time. Rather it would become the lead focal institution for change.

CONCLUSION

It is not easy to cope with change. Change brings about pressure to do things in different ways and a break away from established practices and habits. Learning new behaviour and adopting new attitudes are required. These are not easy propositions. These are a few of the many reasons as to why changes are resisted and not implemented.

Experiences of the Commonwealth countries have demonstrated that significant changes can be brought about and sustained in the public service provided there is political commitment to do so. Other variables that are also important include credibility of the reform programme, designating a focal point for change exercise, ownership of reforms by public servants, enhancing consumer expectation, instituting systems of feedback, building support for change outside and acceptance of change as a continuous activity.

A number of recommendations have been made to reform the public service in Bangladesh. Many of the recommendations are different from the measures implemented in the Commonwealth countries because the ills that afflict the public bureaucracy are so deep-rooted and fundamental that to overcome these one has to propose wide-ranging change measures of far-reaching consequences. But there are also commonalities. Political will must be the driving force behind a reformed public service in Bangladesh. A sea-change must occur in the orientation and work ethics of public servants. The public service must be accountable for its actions and transparent in its activities. Size of the public sector must be significantly reduced to enable more competition and improvement in the delivery of services. The structure of the public service must be rationalized. Widespread corruption among public servants must be checked by instituting strict anti-corruption measures and enhancing pay and emoluments of public servants based on their performance. Training and indoctrination systems need to be reorganized to equip the public servants with necessary knowledge and skills as well as to contribute changes in their beliefs, values and attitudes to enable them to appropriately perform their tasks. Merit-based selection lies at the heart of a competent public service and this has to be ensured. The critical role of the civil society in reform implementation needs to be understood and accorded necessary importance. International donors can and should play a significant role in this regard. At the sametime institutionalizing a reform implementation body with wide- ranging powers and responsibilities is absolutely vital for successful implementation of major administrative reforms on a continuous basis.

REFERENCES

Commonwealth Secretariat (1995). *From Problem to Solution : Commonwealth Strategies for Reform*. London: Commonwealth Secretariat.

Rahman, M. A. et al. (1993). *Towards Better Government in Bangladesh*. Dhaka : Bangladesh Government Press.

UNDP (1993). *Report on Public Administration Sector Study in Bangladesh*. New York : United Nations Development Programme.

World Bank, the (1996a). *Government that Works: Reforming the Public Sector*. Washington, D.C. : the World Bank.

World Bank, the (1996b). *Bangladesh: An Agenda for Action*. Washington, D.C.: The World Bank.

Index